Becoming MAN

Study Guide

Developing the Prophet, Priest, King and Warrior Within

by IV Marsh

*I am about to go the way of all the earth.
Be strong, and show yourself a man.*

1 Kings 2:2

Copyright © 2018 by IV Marsh

Requests for information should be addressed to:

Email: info@iam4.tv

ISBN 978-1-723-02414-6

All Scripture quotations, unless otherwise indicated, are taken from The Holy Bible, New International Version®, NIV®. Copyright © 1973, 1978, 1984, 2011 by Biblica, Inc.® All rights reserved worldwide. www.Zondervan.com. The "NIV" and "New International Version" are trademarks registered in the United States Patent and Trademark Office by Biblica, Inc.®

Scripture quotations marked ESV are taken from the ESV® Bible (The Holy Bible, English Standard Version®). Copyright © 2001 by Crossway, a publishing ministry of Good News Publishers. Used by permission. All rights reserved.

Scripture quotations marked KJV are taken from the King James Version. Public domain.

Scripture quotations marked MSG [or The Message] are taken from *The Message*. Copyright © by Eugene H. Peterson 1993, 1994, 1995, 1996, 2000, 2001, 2002. Used by permission of NavPress. All rights reserved. Represented by Tyndale House Publishers, Inc.

Scripture quotations marked NKJV are taken from the New King James Version®. © 1982 by Thomas Nelson. All rights reserved.

Scripture quotations marked NLT are taken from the Holy Bible, New Living Translation. © 1996, 2004, 2007, 2013, 2015 by Tyndale House Foundation. All rights reserved.

Any internet addresses (websites, blogs, etc.) and telephone numbers in this book are offered as a resource. They are not intended in any way to be or imply an endorsement by IV Marsh, nor does IV Marsh vouch for the content of these sites and numbers for the life of this book.

All rights reserved. No part of this publication may be reproduced, stored in a retrieval system, or transmitted in any form or by any means—electronic, mechanical, photocopy, recording, or any other—except for brief quotations in printed reviews, without the prior permission of the publisher.

First printing 2018 / Printed in the United States of America.

Contents

About the Author

Introduction How to Use This Bible Study

Week 1   Show Yourself A Man

    Day 1 Be Masculine
    Day 2 Acquire Wisdom
    Day 3 See Jesus Correctly
    Day 4 Understand Legacy
    Day 5 Build Your Own Legacy
    Day 6 Become a True Man
    Day 7 Recognize the Problems of Society

Week 2   Our Greatest Struggles

    Day 1 Believe Right So You Can Live Right
    Day 2 Imitate Christ
    Day 3 Recognize Three Common Weaknesses
    Day 4 Defeat Passiveness
    Day 5 Overcome Aggressiveness
    Day 6 Correct Misguided Self-Depreciation
    Day 7 Take the Cure

Week 3   Becoming a Priest

    Day 1 Be A Servant
    Day 2 Take Practical Steps
    Day 3 Be Salt and Light
    Day 4 Understand The 4 Steps
    Day 5 Take Responsibility
    Day 6 Step Up
    Day 7 Pray

Week 4   Becoming a Warrior

    Day 1 Deal With Doubt And Unbelief
    Day 2 Get Mentally Tough
    Day 3 Gain Emotional Control
    Day 4 Be Self-Aware
    Day 5 Get Physically Fit
    Day 6 Develop a Never Quit Attitude
    Day 7 Develop Your Non-negotiables

Week 5   **Becoming a Prophet**

        Day 1   Be Obedient
        Day 2   Examine Your Heart
        Day 3   Begin to Study the Bible
        Day 4   Study the Relationship Between Ideas
        Day 5   Learn How to Interpret Passages
        Day 6   Apply the Word to Your Life
        Day 7   Become a Teacher

Week 6   **Becoming a King**

        Day 1   Communicate Your Vision
        Day 2   Lead Your Home
        Day 3   Judge Wisely
        Day 4   Manage Your Money Well
        Day 5   Eliminate A Poverty Mindset
        Day 6   Break Financial Curses
        Day 7   You Choose: Poverty or Prosperity

About the Author

IV Marsh is a pastor, entrepreneur and leadership coach. He leads Epic Church, a mega multi-site church with his wife, Bené. Epic was planted in 2007. The online campus reaches an additional 5,000 people weekly in multiple countries. IV is the founder and CEO of LeadNow, an organization committed to inspiring and equipping leaders, and IAM4, a men's movement. Recently he launched Warrior Evolution—a week-long intensive that empowers men in spirit, soul and body. A native of North Alabama, IV served in the Air Force and then in law enforcement before stepping into full-time ministry. IV and Bene' have been married for 24 years and have three children and one daughter-in-law.

How to Use This Bible Study

Every man, regardless of his family of origin, baggage or education, is destined to be a Prophet, Priest, King and Warrior in the earth—and that includes you. When you understand, know and fully believe in this—in who God created you to be—the living and doing of it will take care of itself. It will be an outflow of your life.

Thank you for having the courage to take a journey where you will discover who you are created to be in the earth—where you will discover your true identity and develop the prophet, priest, king, and warrior inside. On this journey, I won't be giving you a list of things to do to become a man, but rather I will run alongside you.

I have designed this study guide not to be done alone, but within a tribe of men—together—so that discussions can be had, so that goals can be set, so that you can achieve in a community of accountability to walk in who you were created to be, destroying the goals you set.

The truths and concepts in the pages to follow are not just words on a page or a philosophy to be agreed with, but they are life-altering principles for you to put into practice to unleash the prophet, priest, king and warrior within you.

IV Marsh
Founder of IAM4 & Lead Pastor of Epic Church

WEEK ONE

Show Yourself A Man

"To be fully alive requires knowing what you'd be willing to die for. Until you clarify that, life is motion without meaning."
– Max Venator

King David was a man who portrayed the good, the bad and the ugly. He was an extraordinary king who operated as a priest, valiant warrior and wise prophet—just like we're going to learn to do in this study. On top of being highly developed in his inner man in these roles, he was an accomplished musician, a skilled author, a man of great wisdom, and had once been a dutiful shepherd over his father's flock when he was just a boy. David was courageous and passionate, but also flawed. He achieved greatness in his lifetime and experienced deep sorrows from his horrific mistakes. But God himself summed up David's legacy in one powerful statement: "I have found David the son of Jesse a man after my own heart" (Acts 13:22).

In the account of creation in Genesis 1, the legacy of God the creator is revealed. God created our universe to expand at a rate of speed that cannot be measured. Think about how fast his words, *"Let there be light,"* caused light to be. But of all that God created, humanity brought God the most joy. *"We, out of all creation, became his prized possession" (James 1:18, NLT).* Humanity—man and woman—is God's masterpiece (Ephesians 2:10). Humanity is his true legacy—the glory of God (1 Corinthians 11:7).

Every man has the potential to reveal the characteristics of God to the world. To become a man, fully, and to leave a legacy. David's legacy was being "a man after God's own heart," and as he was dying, his last recorded words were spoken to his son, Solomon: *"I am about to go the way of all the earth.* **Be strong, and show yourself a man,"** (1 Kings 2:2, emphasis added).

Out of all the things David, the greatest king to ever live, could have said, the last words he ever spoke were, *"I'm about to go the way of all the earth. Be strong and show yourself a man."*

David told his son to pay attention to what God says, to honor God, worship God, and put God first—all of which are very important commands. But his parting words, the ones of utmost importance, the ones he didn't want his son to ever forget, were, **"Show yourself a man."**

David didn't tell Solomon to obey the ten commandments and be pure and holy and study all the wisdom he'd written for the ages. No. Of all he could have said, he deemed it most important to basically say, "I am about to die. Be strong and show yourself a man. Do not whine, complain, or make excuses, but be strong. Show everyone around you that you have become a man! That you are a true man!"

Day 1   Be Masculine

When I became a husband, and then a father, I had no idea how enormous that responsibility was. I was taught, like many men, that if I had a good job, provided for my family and maintained the yard, then that made me a good husband and dad. I did that exact thing for years and could not understand why my marriage and children were not flourishing the way I wanted.

What I didn't understand was really how to be a man—and I find that too many men don't understand either. Manhood and masculinity are disappearing before our very eyes. By masculine, I don't mean a man that has muscles on top of muscles and can grow a really good beard. A masculine man, a man's man, is a man who not only demonstrates the physical qualities of ruggedness, but who also possesses mental toughness and emotional strength. A man who says what he means and means what he says. A man who recognizes the importance of honesty. A man of noble principle. A man without covetousness. A man who cannot be bribed or bullied. A man committed to manly virtues. A man who is the head of his home and knows how to love and discipline his children. A man who loves justice but also knows tenderness and mercy. A man who fears God and shows reverence for that which is sacred. A man who knows the difference between the rule of law and the lust for power. On the whole, our society today has little tolerance for such men. Even in our churches, masculinity is dying.

It's overwhelming to think we could make a difference—that we can change all of this, but I believe we can. By learning who God created us to be and how to live that in our personal lives, in our professional lives, in our homes and communities. I believe we can reverse the current trend in culture.

Based on the description I painted, do you feel you are appropriately masculine?

_____

_____

_____

In what ways might you increase your expressions of masculinity?

_____

_____

_____

_____

Why do you think some men struggle with expressing masculine traits?

_____

_____

_____

How can you be of help to men who struggle? How would you coach them in showing themselves a man?

_____

_____

_____

Words to live by: *"I am about to go the way of all the earth. Be strong, and show yourself a man," (1 Kings 2:2).*

Day 2   Acquire Wisdom

Life is not easy, so there is no need to make it any harder than it has to be, but it seems that's what so many of us do. We search and search, reading book after book and blog after blog, trying to figure out how to do life, have a healthy marriage, make friends, and be successful, when it really all boils down to good ol' common sense.

Common sense can be defined as sound judgment based on a simple perception of the situation or facts that everyone should know. You have to earn it, but most of us don't want to go through the necessary process to earn it.

The book of Proverbs is a book of common sense. It is a book of wisdom regarding friendships, moral purity, finances, even marriage. I whole-heartedly recommend reading through Proverbs once a year.

How would you define common sense?

_____

_____

_____

Why do you think some people have it and some don't?

_____

_____

_____

Which book of the Bible should we read to increase our common sense?

_____

_____

_____

Words to live by: *"The beginning of wisdom is this: Get wisdom. Though it cost all you have, get understanding" (Proverbs 4:7, NIV).*

Day 3   See Jesus Correctly

Jesus was a carpenter—a laborer who worked with his hands and lifted heavy chunks of stone and wood daily. His hands had to be calloused and scarred from everyday work. Yes, he was the son of God, but the Word tells us he was fully man (John 1:14). Jesus wasn't just male—he walked in the fullness of true manhood. He knew what it meant to be a man. In fact, he was the perfect man.

Jesus taught his followers that there are things worth fighting for and dying for as men. In Luke 22:36, Jesus told his followers to sell their cloaks and buy swords. He was preparing them for their journey to do his work and establish the church. He was imparting to them wisdom for the days ahead.

And they understood. If necessary, his followers were willing to pay the ultimate sacrifice. Unbeknownst to them, he would demonstrate this passionate lifestyle when he would be nailed to the cross for all of us.

Jesus was never a weak man. In Matthew 21, he walked into the temple in Jerusalem and became righteously angry at people selling their wares in the temple. He turned over the tables of the moneychangers and the benches of those selling doves. He chased people out of the temple, accusing them of turning his house of prayer into a den of robbers. He was angry at them because they were dishonoring God.

Jesus was zealous and bold in his pursuit and defense of God the Father. The character of Jesus was tough and rugged, yet also loving and compassionate. Jesus portrayed a beautiful balance of humility and power for us. To discover what it really means to be a man, we must be willing to embrace the true Jesus as our savior and role model for manhood.

Be honest. What was your image of Jesus when you were growing up?

_____

_____

_____

What is your image of Jesus now?

_____

_____

_____

_____

What shaped your image of Jesus? Culture? The Church? Your parents?

_____

_____

_____

How have you defined Jesus to your children (if you are a father)?

_____

_____

_____

Does understanding he was a carpenter, told his followers to buy swords, got angry, and confronted religious bigots alter your image of Jesus?

_____

_____

_____

Words to live by: *"For those God foreknew he also predestined to be conformed to the image of his Son, that he might be the firstborn among many brothers and sisters" (Romans 8:29).*

Day 4   Understand Legacy

Where did Jesus learn to be a man? Yes, I know he was God, but he came to earth fully man. Who taught him? Joseph, we assume. But where did Joseph and all the men of his day learn? The same place we can. From the Word of God.

In Jesus' day, men read from The Old Testament, and one of the greatest leaders his father Joseph would have learned from and taught Jesus about was King David.

As I said earlier, David's legacy was being "a man after God's own heart," and as he was dying, his last recorded words were spoken to his son, Solomon: *"I am about to go the way of all the earth.* ***Be strong, and show yourself a man,"*** (1 Kings 2:2).

Every man has the potential to reveal the characteristics of God to the world. To become a man, fully, and to leave a legacy.

What legacy are you leaving behind?

_____

_____

_____

_____

What will other people say about you after you have left this earth?

_____

_____

_____

_____

What do you want them to say?

_____

_____

_____

_____

Out of all the things David, the greatest king to ever live, could have said, the last words he ever spoke were, *"I'm about to go the way of all the earth. Be strong and show yourself a man."* I can't help but think if I were breathing my last breath, and I was going to get to speak only one last thought to my two sons, what would I say? What would you say to yours?

_____

_____

_____

_____

Words to live by: *"A good man leaves an inheritance to his children's children..." (Proverbs 13:22, KJV).*

Day 5   Build Your Own Legacy

If David made it so clear to Solomon, to show himself a man, and it's been in the Bible for us in our lifetimes, why haven't we all been raised with this truth?

_____

_____

_____

Why do so many men fail to understand what it means to truly "show yourself a man" in every aspect of their lives—personally, privately, professionally, and publicly?

_____

_____

_____

How can we hold one another accountable and help one another show ourselves a man and teach others how to live this way?

_____

_____

_____

Words to live by: *"We will not keep them from our children; we will tell the next generation about the Lord 's power and his great deeds and the wonderful things he has done" (Psalms 78:4 GNB).*

Day 6   Become a True Man

David wanted Solomon to understand and live as the kind of man who makes a family whole, a woman feel safe, a child confident, and a community strong. He wanted him to be a man rooted in honor and devotion.

A true man is always aware.

A true man never fails to mind the territory he's been given or wear the responsibility with which it has been entrusted.

A true man guards, protects, and reflects the heart of God and the life of Jesus.

How have you embraced responsibility in your lifetime?

_____

_____

_____

Have there been times when you have deflected your responsibilities?

_____

_____

_____

Are there amends you need to make?

_____

_____

_____

How can you live even more honorably that you are now?

_____

_____

_____

Words to live by: *"The Lord knows the days of the upright and blameless, and their heritage will abide forever" (Psalm 37:18 AMP).*

Day 7   Recognize the Problems of Society

It doesn't matter what modern-day writings and research you read; it is conclusive that where men (fathers) are absent, culture is torn apart at the seams. Psychology Today explained this issue thoroughly:

> Researchers have found that for children, the results are nothing short of disastrous, along a number of dimensions:
>
> *–children's diminished self-concept, and compromised physical and emotional security* (children consistently report feeling abandoned when their fathers are not involved in their lives, struggling with their emotions and episodic bouts of self-loathing)
>
> *–behavioral problems* (fatherless children have more difficulties with social adjustment, and are more likely to report problems with friendships, and manifest behavior problems; many develop a swaggering, intimidating persona in an attempt to disguise their underlying fears, resentments, anxieties, and unhappiness)
>
> *–truancy and poor academic performance* (71 percent of high school dropouts are fatherless; fatherless children have more trouble academically, scoring poorly on tests of reading, mathematics, and thinking skills; children from father absent homes are more likely to play truant from school, more likely to be excluded from school, more likely to leave school at age 16, and less likely to attain academic and professional qualifications in adulthood)
>
> *–delinquency and youth crime, including violent crime* (85 percent of youth in prison have an absent father; fatherless children are more likely to offend and go to jail as adults)
>
> *–promiscuity and teen pregnancy* (fatherless children are more likely to experience problems with sexual health, including a greater likelihood of having intercourse before the age of 16, foregoing contraception during first intercourse, becoming teenage parents, and contracting sexually transmitted infection; girls manifest an object hunger for males, and in experiencing the emotional loss of their fathers egocentrically as a rejection of them, become susceptible to exploitation by adult men)
>
> *–drug and alcohol abuse* (fatherless children are more likely to smoke, drink alcohol, and abuse drugs in childhood and adulthood)
>
> *–homelessness* (90 percent of runaway children have an absent father)
>
> *–exploitation and abuse* (fatherless children are at greater risk of suffering physical, emotional, and sexual abuse, being five times more likely to have experienced physical abuse and emotional maltreatment, with a one hundred times higher risk of fatal abuse; a recent study reported that preschoolers not living with both of their biological parents are 40 times more likely to be sexually abused)

—physical health problems (fatherless children report significantly more psychosomatic health symptoms and illness such as acute and chronic pain, asthma, headaches, and stomach aches)

—mental health disorders (father-absent children are consistently overrepresented on a wide range of mental health problems, particularly anxiety, depression, and suicide)

—life chances (as adults, fatherless children are more likely to experience unemployment, have low incomes, remain on social assistance, and experience homelessness)

—future relationships (father-absent children tend to enter partnerships earlier, are more likely to divorce or dissolve their cohabiting unions, and are more likely to have children outside marriage or outside any partnership)

—mortality (fatherless children are more likely to die as children and live an average of four years less over the life span) Given the fact that these and other social problems correlate more strongly with fatherlessness than with any other factor, surpassing race, social class and poverty, father absence may well be the most critical social issue of our time.

https://www.psychologytoday.com/us/blog/co-parenting-after-divorce/201205/father-absence-father-deficit-father-hunger

In light of this article, in what ways did you experience fatherlessness—even if your father was around?

_____

_____

_____

How can you be a stronger father to your children?

_____

_____

_____

How can you be a stronger father figure to other young men?

_____

_____

_____

What can we do as a corporate group of men to help young men have a father figure?

_____

_____

_____

Words to live by: *"Fathers, do not exasperate your children; instead, bring them up in the training and instruction of the Lord" (Ephesians 6:4).*

WEEK TWO

Our Greatest Struggles

"The ultimate measure of a man is not where he stands in a moment of comfort or convenience, but where he stands at times of challenge and controversy."
– Martin Luther King, Jr.

There are forces fighting against us on every level—forces designed to pull us into places mentally, emotionally and spiritually where we won't succeed. And those forces have been battling for our manhood since the story of Creation in the Garden of Eden.

When God created man, he came to the conclusion that it was not good for man to be alone, so he created woman, and that led to his divine plan of family (Genesis 2). The two essential elements of family are marriage and parenthood.

Marriage and parenthood reveal God's character like nothing else in creation. The love between a husband and wife provides a glimpse of Christ's passionate devotion to his bride—the Church. In the same way, the ups and downs of parenthood offer a compelling representation of God's tenderness and patience toward his children.

Even Christ himself was born within the context of a family. Jesus submitted to an earthly mother and father in order to model what it means to honor parents and to benefit from their loving direction and guidance. It was within the nurturing care of Christ's earthly family that *"Jesus grew in wisdom and stature, and in favor with God and man"* (Luke 2:52).

We are created and called to follow this divine order: *"Therefore be imitators of God, as beloved children; and walk in love, just as Christ also loved you and gave Himself up for us, an offering and a sacrifice to God as a fragrant aroma"* (Ephesians 5:1-2).

We were created to imitate God, our Father, who created us in his own image. When Jesus walked the earth, he demonstrated this perfectly for us—so we could succeed in imitating him in all that we are and all that we do. And yet, we battle in this assignment. Why? Because we were all born into sin; therefore, as Romans 3:23 reminds us, we all fall short of displaying God's glory.

That is why God sent his only Son, Jesus, to die for our sin. When Jesus left the earth, God sent his Holy Spirit to empower us to live out our God-given potential free from the chains of sin and death. We still face sin in this fallen world, but as Christ-followers, we were given the power to overcome sin.

But in the meantime, we battle.

Day 1 Believe Right So You Can Live Right

"Most people are only in predicaments that they put themselves in," my Papaw once said, "and when you are sick and tired of being sick and tired most of the time, you're the only one that can get you out. The good news is once a man has made up his mind to do something, all he's left to do is do it. But can't nobody do it for you."

In other words, you cannot live differently than you believe. Proverbs 23:7 says, *"For as a man thinks within himself so he is."*

Everyone is one decision away from a different life. It is too easy to blame our current situation on people and circumstances, but we fail to see the common denominator in all of life situations–ourselves. If you want to change your life, you must change what you believe. If you want a different life, then you must make the decision to change the way you live.

How do you perceive yourself? As a victim? As a leader? As successful? As a failure?

_____

_____

_____

How does what you think daily affect your perspective?

_____

_____

_____

Isn't what you think what you believe?

_____

_____

_____

To change what you believe, you will have to change what you think. How can you do that?

_____

_____

_____

Words to live by: *"Do not conform to the pattern of this world, but be transformed by the renewing of your mind. Then you will be able to test and approve what God's will is-- his good, pleasing and perfect will" (Romans 12:2).*

Day 2 Imitate Christ

Christ himself was born within the context of a family. Jesus submitted to an earthly mother and father in order to model what it means to honor parents and to benefit from their loving direction and guidance. It was within the nurturing care of Christ's earthly family that *"Jesus grew in wisdom and stature, and in favor with God and man" (Luke 2:52).*

We are created and called to follow this divine order: *"Therefore be imitators of God, as beloved children; and walk in love, just as Christ also loved you and gave Himself up for us, an offering and a sacrifice to God as a fragrant aroma" (Ephesians 5:1-2).*

We were created to imitate God, our Father, who created us in his own image. When Jesus walked the earth, he demonstrated this perfectly for us—so we could succeed in imitating him in all that we are and all that we do. And yet, we battle in this assignment. Why? Because we were all born into sin; therefore, as Romans 3:23 reminds us, we all fall short of displaying God's glory.

Describe a time when you fell short, when you were disappointed in yourself?

_____

_____

_____

Did you ask God to forgive you?

_____

_____

_____

Did you ask others to forgive you if you sinned against them?

_____

_____

_____

Did you forgive yourself?

_____

_____

Forgiving yourself is part of being an imitator of God, of submitting to God's authority. To not forgive ourselves is to put ourselves in God's place.

_____

_____

_____

Words to live by: *"I have swept away your offenses like a cloud, your sins like the morning mist. Return to me, for I have redeemed you" (Isaiah 44:22).*

Day 3 Recognize Three Common Weaknesses

When Jesus left the earth, God sent his Holy Spirit to empower us to live out our God-given potential free from the chains of sin and death. We still face sin in this fallen world, but as Christ-followers, we were given the power to overcome sin.

But in the meantime, we battle. I have found, as I've walked men to the place of truly showing themselves a man in every area of their lives, that our inability to imitate Christ can often be rooted in one of three weaknesses in our lives: either extreme passiveness, aggressiveness or misguided self-depreciation.

Having read the book, define passiveness:

_____

_____

_____

Define aggressiveness:

_____

_____

_____

Define misguided self-depreciation:

_____

_____

_____

Words to live by: *"But when he, the Spirit of truth, comes, he will guide you into all the truth. He will not speak on his own; he will speak only what he hears, and he will tell you what is yet to come" (John 16:13).*

Day 4   Defeat Passiveness

Like any character trait, being passive isn't always wrong or detrimental. Sometimes the best course of action is to let something "roll off your back." There are those situations where it's best to be silent or simply walk away. But I have found that for a true man, that is the exception, not the rule.

When we choose to be silent and a voice is needed, our silence and passivity become sin. *"If anyone, then, knows the good they ought to do and doesn't do it, it is sin for them" (James 4:17).* No man ever wants to admit this, but being passive at the wrong time is clearly sin.

What is your natural tendency? To be passive or to speak up?

_____

_____

_____

Why do you think you remain silent at times when you should speak up?

_____

_____

_____

Do you find that you avoid conflict? Or see it as necessary to reach resolve?

_____

_____

_____

In what areas of your life do you need to speak up more?

_____

_____

_____

Words to live by: *"If anyone, then, knows the good they ought to do and doesn't do it, it is sin for them" (James 4:17).*

Day 5   Overcome Aggressiveness

All men struggle with sinful aggressiveness. It is why men stand around and make fun of people. It is why men withhold affection and attention from someone who fails them. They utilize power, money and education to manipulate people and circumstances. They are sarcastic and do not mind inflicting pain on others. They alienate their family and cause everyone to walk on eggshells.

His wife avoids any hint of conflict—but not because she respects him and is sensitive to how tired he is. No. She is afraid of him. The last time she tried to get him to do something around the house, the abuse was too much. Whether it was a verbal lashing or a physical beating, she is equally afraid of both. He feels entitled, just like his passive counterpart, but his reasons are different. He provides for his family. He has sacrificed his life to provide a nice home, nice clothes, nice cars, and week-long vacations for his family. His attitude is that no one better disrespect him in HIS house, and if someone does disrespect him, they will pay for it.

But do they really respect him?

Have you ever been guilty of causing your wife or children to fear you?

_____

_____

_____

Does your family—or others—truly respect you?

_____

_____

_____

How do you know?

_____

_____

_____

How can you hold your aggressiveness in check?

___

___

___

Words to live by: *"My dear brothers and sisters, take note of this: Everyone should be quick to listen, slow to speak and slow to become angry, because human anger does not produce the righteousness that God desires" James 1:19-20).*

Day 6   Correct Misguided Self-Depreciation

This behavioral trait is often confused with humility. In an attempt to appear humble, a man like this will wrongly judge who he is and how God created him to be and then act out of it living a lesser role than God intended. A role that can become depressive and sinful.

How many of these self-depreciating patterns apply to you?

- ☐ Volunteering in the community or church, and people thinking you're a "nice guy," but truthfully, you are pitied.
- ☐ Your view of life is that it "sucks." Your self-esteem is extremely low, and you constantly struggle with depression.
- ☐ You get counseling repeatedly for the same sins year after year.
- ☐ Your wife stays with you out of fear that you will commit suicide—although truth be told, she's so emotionally bankrupt that while she may stay physically, she already has one foot out the door by having either an emotional or physical affair.
- ☐ Your children have no respect for you and feel abandoned by their father.
- ☐ If you are single, perhaps you find yourself incapable of maintaining a relationship with the opposite sex. Deep down you don't feel you deserve one.
- ☐ To compensate, you immerse yourself in volunteer roles.
- ☐ There is never a good day and you are always "just getting by."
- ☐ Other_____

Words to live by: *"Do not let anyone who delights in false humility and the worship of angels disqualify you. Such a person also goes into great detail about what they have seen; they are puffed up with idle notions by their unspiritual mind" (Colossians 2:18).*

Day 7   Take the Cure

What are the four roles Jesus lived that we are to emulate in our lives?

1. _____

2. _____

3. _____

4. _____

As the ultimate revelation of _____, Jesus represents us fully to the Father and brings the supreme atoning sacrifice—himself—that appeases the Father's holy and just wrath against us for our sin.

Jesus was prophesied to be a _____ in the Old Testament (Exodus 15:3). And it is foreshadowed, that at the end of the age, he will return on a white horse showing himself as a _____ (Revelations 19:11-16).

As the _____, Jesus speaks the Word of God to us. *"When you have lifted up the Son of Man, then you will know that I am he and that I do nothing on my own but speak just what the Father has taught me"* (John 8:28).

As a _____ king, he is the conquering and reigning King, forever worthy of our worship and adoration. He is the King of Kings and Lord of Lords—the one with absolute dominion over all his realm, whom no one can oppose or defeat (Revelation 19:16).

Understanding Jesus' roles and how we are to imitate these roles in our lives is essential to showing ourselves a man. And no matter how well we have succeeded at these roles or failed, Christ made a way for us and all of our years to be redeemed—but to experience the benefits of his redemption, we must be born again. Have you surrendered your life to God? Have you placed your faith in the sacrifice of Jesus and his finished work on the cross?

If you haven't, pray this prayer and surrender your life to him fully:

God in Heaven, I have lived my life in sinfulness. I have not stepped into my role as a man. I have sinned and fallen short of your glory. I place my faith in Jesus' sacrifice and His finished work on the cross, repenting (turning away) from that life and turning to You. I also believe that Jesus rose from the dead on the third day defeating sin and death.

I ask you to forgive me of my sin and redeem me so that I may walk in the life you have for me. Thank you, Father, for saving me! God fill me with your Holy Spirit, empowering me to live out my creative order as a man. Amen!

Words to live by: *"For God so loved the world that he gave his one and only Son, that whoever believes in him shall not perish but have eternal life" (John 3:16).*

WEEK THREE

Becoming a Priest

"The man who is deserving the name is the one whose thoughts and exertions are for others rather than for himself."
—Walter Scott

As priest, Jesus came to earth and bore the weight of our sin and shame on the cross. He gave the ultimate sacrifice by dying for all the sins of all humanity. Then he was buried and rose again, being seated at the right hand of the Father where he continues to intercede for us. He was a bridge, a mediator, called to intercede in the Lord's presence on behalf of the people. He prepared a way for us to approach God and experience God.

Our role in imitating him isn't to die a physical death as he did, but it is to die to ourselves—to our flesh and its demanding desires—especially when we're tempted to sin and be passive, aggressive or self-depreciating. It's to be a bridge, a mediator, for our families, friends, co-workers, and community leaders, to intercede in the Lord's presence on behalf of everyone in our circle of influence. To act like Jesus is to step in as an advocate who presents himself as a representative for another.

Day 1   Be a Servant

As Priest, we are called to serve others and serve God's house. Most often we find that less than 20 percent of individuals who call a church their home actually serve the church in any capacity. As you study this office of Christ and your divine role of priest, examine your life.

Are you serving other people and serving the church you call home?

_____

_____

_____

Who takes the lead in serving in your home today?

_____

_____

_____

In **Matthew 21**, Jesus told a story with an important point:

"What do you think? There was a man who had two sons. He went to the first and said, 'Son, go and work today in the vineyard.'
"'I will not,' he answered, but later he changed his mind and went.
"Then the father went to the other son and said the same thing. He answered, 'I will, sir,' but he did not go.
"Which of the two did what his father wanted?" (verses 28-31)

If you were standing with Jesus on this day how would you have answered his question?

_____

_____

_____

This story is the tale of 2 sons: **Son #1** who is a punk, and **Son #2,** the one with his hair parted and dressed in Vineyard Vines.® The question for you is this: Will you be more like **Son #1** who said, "No," but later changed his mind and did as his father asked? Or **Son #2** who said, "Yes," but never did as the father requested?

Our intentions to do well have a tendency to fade because we make compassion much too complicated.

Jesus speaking in **Matthew 5:14-16** said, *"You are the light of the world, a city on a hill cannot be hidden neither do people light a lamp and put it under a bowl instead they put it on a stand and it gives light to everyone in the house. In the same way let your light shine before others that they may see your good deeds and glorify your Father in Heaven."*

He is saying to us, when it comes to getting the message out to this jaded uninterested world, about the only thing people pay attention to is compassion. Not words, works, good intentions, but rather true and genuine compassion.

So, Jesus says to us: Go ahead and build your churches, come up with your mission statement for your church, and your 12-year strategic plan on seeing 12,000 in 12 years. But don't forget that at the base of who you are—you are salt and light.

Real impact takes place when you see a need and meet a need. Vision and plans to make those visions a reality are a must; however, they must always be wrapped in love and compassion for those we meet along the way.

Where has God revealed to you a need for genuine compassion in your home, life and church?

What is holding you back from stepping in and at least getting things moving in these situations?

Helen Keller said, *"I am only one, but still I am one. I cannot do everything, but still I can do something. I will not refuse to do the something I can do."* She is saying that change comes to the world **one life at a time.**

The principle of living in compassion and the foundation of spiritual transformation is, *"We move from good intentions to real life change when we make and keep small specific commitments."*

What commitments have you made that you need to follow through on?

_____

_____

_____

Words to live by: *"Let your light so shine before people that they would get to know God" (Matthew 5:16).*

Day 2   Take Practical Steps

4 Steps to take that help you serve as you serve.

1. **LIVE - Start in your world.**

In the story of Peter and John healing the lame man at the temple in Acts 3, Peter and John were aware of their surroundings. They noticed the things around them. Yes, they had a plan, a mission for the morning; however, the plan was not more important than the people God placed in their path. Also, Peter and John did not make excuses for what they did NOT have, and instead, they leveraged what they had been given. The result was a lame man was healed, not because Peter and John were super special, but rather because they simply accessed the power placed within them.

Anne Frank said: *"How wonderful it is that nobody need wait a single minute before starting to improve the world."*

God put you where you are for a reason and has given you amazing gifts to use in serving others.

Who has God placed in your life that you have looked past because you have felt inadequate or that helping them could interrupt your plans?

_____

_____

_____

2. **SEE - Ask God to open your eyes so you can see the needs all around you.**

In Matthew 25:31-46, Jesus tells the story of the sheep and the goats. Those listening to Jesus were challenged with the reality that they had opportunity to serve Him but did not. They pushed back on His conclusion to which Jesus indicated that when they did not feed, clothe, visit and care for their fellow man, they did not care for Him. We must understand that God loves all mankind, and when we choose to ignore those He puts in our path, that truthfully, we are ignoring Him. We are most like Christ when we are serving the most valuable He died for—mankind.

Replay your past week. Who did God put in your path that you did not see?

_____

_____

_____

3. LOVE - Ask God what you should do for others. Love is a verb!

Ask yourself: "Is there some simple act of love I could perform today that will change a life?" Capture what you hear below.

_____

_____

_____

Matthew 10:41 (MSG) *"This is a large work I've called you into. But don't be overwhelmed by it. It's best to start small, give a cool cup of water to someone who is thirsty for instance. The smallest act of giving or receiving makes you a true apprentice. You won't lose out on a thing."*

Although it appears to be a very large task for us, Jesus says not to get overwhelmed because it is as easy as offering someone a cup of water.

Mother Teresa once said, *"If you can't feed a hundred people, then feed just one."* The world is not changed by building church buildings, or having great church music, or having preachers with Mohawks. The world is changed one person at a time as you give a simple cup of cold water. When we decide that we are going to change the "ones" God has placed in our lives, real change will begin to happen.

What are a few simple ways you can express the love of God to others around you today?

_____

_____

_____

4. RALLY - Thank God you have a church that has your back.

Williams Woodsworth once said: *"This is the best portion of a good man's life; his little nameless unremembered acts of kindness and love."*

Are you doing your part?

When you are asked to volunteer in the children's department or out in the parking lot, your serving is not designed to make you feel better. You are asked so that an amazing experience can be created in the local church on Sunday that reaches out into our communities. You know when you are asked to give financially, it is not to run the business of the church, but rather you give to the church so it has the resources needed to be an epicenter of impact all over the world. As we rally together, we can have confidence, knowing that if needs arise, the church has each and every one of our backs. But this can only happen successfully if each one of us are doing our part.

Doing your part is a simple, but oftentimes difficult, step. However, it demonstrates that you have more than strong feelings, more than good intentions, more than religious sentiment for people. It indicates that you are not just a son who says all the right things at the breakfast table, and never shows up at the vineyard, but that you are truly committed to the master.

What is your next step in our spiritual journey? If you do not know, then talk to your pastor or male leader of your church?

_____

_____

_____

What part of "your part" is currently not being done today?

_____

_____

_____

Words to live by: *"…whatever you did for one of the least of these brothers and sisters of mine, you did for me'" (Matthew 25:40).*

Day 3   Be Salt and Light

We are referred to as Salt and Light in a tasteless and dark world, and we are called to bring flavor and light to those around us. God did not call us out of the darkness to immediately disconnect from people. In Romans 12, Paul tells us we are to be in the world, but not of the world. In other words, we are to connect with those in the world who are hurting and broken, but not live as they live. The truth is we most often pull back from the world and people because they have issues, and we feel inadequate to address them. We are aware that we have our own issues walking our spiritual journey, and so we judge ourselves unworthy to guide others. But the truth is we were not made to hide the light God placed inside us. We were made to allow our light to shine bright.

Matthew 5:14-16: *"You are the light of the world, a city on a hill cannot be hidden neither do people light a lamp and put it under a bowl instead they put it on a stand and it gives light to everyone in the house. In the same way let your light shine before others that they may see your good deeds and glorify your Father in Heaven."*

The reality is that broken people are all around us in our world and in our cities. And those people need men to take their place as priests, being light in very dark places. We need to take the light to every area of life we function in, and we need to take the light to every place God leads us. We are to be light in our homes, workplaces, communities, and churches. The souls of the broken and hurting are screaming out for us to be the true priests God created us to be. We're not to be men afraid of a little hard, dirty work, but men who see the opportunity to share truth and power with every individual God allows us to meet.

With the above being true, what are needs God has placed in front of you where your light needs to shine?

_____

_____

_____

Will you be part of the solution or act like these things are not happening? What will you do to make a difference today?

_____

_____

_____

Words to live by: *"You are the salt of the earth. But if the salt loses its saltiness, how can it be made salty again? It is no longer good for anything, except to be thrown out and trampled underfoot" (Matthew 5:13).*

Day 4   Understand the 4 Steps

As we discovered last week there are 4 steps to take which will help us serve those around us. As a reminder, they are:

- Live - Start where you live
- See - The needs around you
- Love - Be activated by love
- Rally - Use the community you're a part of to rally together

Given that we now know the truth and understand the call placed on us as men, we must address a very important verse in James that we all at times wish God had not included in the Bible: *"Anyone, then, who knows the good he should do and doesn't do it, sins" (James 4:17).*

How does this scripture apply to you personally today? Is there something you know to do but are not doing?

_____

_____

_____

Theologians refer to this scripture as positive disobedience. It is the idea that if I have a sense of what is right to do, and I leave it for someone else to do and walk away, then I have violated my own conscience. This sensation usually leads to an emotion we call guilt. However, God tells us in scripture that as Christ-followers there is no longer condemnation for those who believe. But Satan wishes to choke us with our failures or missed opportunities by using guilt and condemnation as a method to control our minds. As Priests, we are to push through our failures and missed opportunities, learning from them in order to not repeat the same behavior. Take some time, put this study down for a few minutes, and ask God to guide you through missed opportunities and failures in your recent past. Ask Him specifically to show you where you missed the mark and how to correct your behavior so you do not repeat the past.

_____

_____

_____

_____

_____

Let's look at a couple of real world scenarios, placing ourselves in the moment, and answering honestly how we would respond:

You are driving down the road, and it is raining. You see someone having car trouble parked on the side of the road. Do you stop and help or keep driving?

_____

_____

_____

Why?

_____

_____

_____

Your wife comes home from shopping, and she is super excited about her purchase, and she asks you what you think of her new headband. It truly is not attractive on her. Do you politely tell her you think it nice or tell her it looks like a crow that has been run over?

_____

_____

_____

Why?

_____

_____

_____

Sometimes it is so hard to know what to do. We know we should take time to help, but we are already on our way to help someone else. We know that if we tell someone the truth, then it will hurt or possibly crush their spirit. But if we are not honest, then they are going to suffer believing a false assumption. We experience real spiritual tension in these moments, so we must rely on the only real voice of truth in our lives.

We must rely on the Holy Spirit to guide us when we feel this tension of "doing the right thing."

In our society, we have seen this tension play out so many times. How often have we heard about a person who was drowning in a pool, lake, river or ocean, and there were several "by-standers" watching the entire tragedy go down before them. The weird thing is that no one did anything other than watch. Everyone maybe called for help but no one actually helped. All the while the person in the water was fading closer and closer toward death. Why did no one jump in the water to save the drowning person? It is not fear, but rather the thought that "someone else will jump in," because deep down they believe "it is someone else's responsibility to jump in." No, it's not. I know this scenario sounds insane, but the practical application of it is true and happens around us all the time. We see people drowning in life's circumstances and situations and do nothing to intervene. Priests are created to take the truth and light to those drowning in all of life's circumstances. We are to speak the truth even if we believe it may "hurt their feelings" or "embarrass them." We are to be light in their dark world.

We are supposed to be a part of the solution. Who do you know today that is drowning?

_____

_____

_____

Maybe it is not just a single person or event, but rather a big issue such as homelessness, starving children in your community, or sexual slavery and trafficking. Are you "calling for help" or are you "jumping in the water?" What science has proven is that in an emergency situation, when one person decides to act, others will follow quickly. As you jump in the water to help those around you who are drowning, you will give others the courage to join the cause and great things will happen. You will not be alone in the cause for long.

Words to live by: *"Therefore, there is now no condemnation for those who are in Christ Jesus" (Romans 8:1).*

Day 5   Take Responsibility

Why do humans in general evade responsibility? Social scientists tell us it is for 2 reasons:

1. The "It's not my fault syndrome" – This is where a person sees a situation and feels no reason to get involved because they see the consequences of the situation as "they brought it on themselves."
2. Bystander Affect - When there is an emergency, the more bystanders there are, the less likely it is that any of them will help.

Research started in the 1960s that proves this point, due to a brutal murder that took place in New York. The murder occurred over a 45-minute period where the murderer left the victim and came back three times and as 38 different people watched it all happen. No one helped, and no one called police. They simply watched in horror and did nothing.

The more people witnessing an event, the less likely anyone is to intervene. Why is this the case?

There are 2 major influences that cause this to happen.

1. <u>Social Influence</u> - Bystanders monitor the reactions of other people in an emergency situation to see if others think that it is necessary to intervene. Since everyone is doing exactly the same thing, which happens to be nothing, then they all conclude from the inaction of others that help is not needed.
2. <u>Diffusion of Responsibility</u> - This occurs when observers all assume that someone else is going to intervene, and so individuals feel less responsible and refrain from doing anything.

And there are other reasons why people may not help:

- They may assume that others are more qualified.
- They assume the intervention would be unneeded or unwelcomed.
- They do not want to look bad.
- They do not want to be injured themselves.

So here is the interesting thing about why humans generally do not get involved. It's not because we are greedy, mean or lack compassion. It is just that simply, we are not willing to assume responsibility for the needs of another person. It is called the Bystander Affect.

The Bystander Affect is a danger of being a part of a large church or organization. It is why on average 20 percent of the people do the work of the church while 80 percent simply watch and complain. It is also why missions to our own communities suffer, but foreign missions are so appealing. If we serve at home, people are more likely to "see us" or "know us" causing us to pull back from the needs close to us. Jesus was very clear on the matter of missions at home or meeting the needs of those close around us.

Matthew 10:5-8, The Message Bible: *"Don't begin by traveling to some far-off place to convert unbelievers. And don't try to be dramatic by tackling some public enemy. Go to the lost, confused people right here in the neighborhood. Tell them that the kingdom is here. Bring health to the sick. Raise the dead. Touch the untouchables. Kick out the demons. You have been treated generously, so live generously."*

Think about that last statement. God intervened in your broken life, so now it's time for you to move out into other people's broken lives. We are to give generously, not because we are special or super spiritual, but rather because God was generous to us. Another translation of this same passage says, "Freely you have received now freely give."

What does it look like for you to freely give?

_____

_____

_____

To whom or what is God calling you today to freely give your time, talents and resources?

_____

_____

_____

_____

Words to live by: *"You have been treated generously, so live generously"* (Matthew 10:8, The Message Bible).

Day 6   Step Up

How do we move from bystanders to actually becoming part of the solution? Here are 5 steps we must take in order to get involved:

1. Notice the event.

John 9:8-10: *"His neighbors and those who had formerly seen him begging asked, 'Isn't this the same man who used to sit and beg?' Some claimed that he was. Others said, 'No, he only looks like him.' But he himself insisted, 'I am the man.'"*
Be in each moment, not overwhelmed by future or past events. We often miss the opportunities right in front of us because we are so consumed with the "next" or "past" event in our lives. God is placing people in your path at every instant for a purpose—in the line at the grocery store, the fast food restaurant, at work, at church, and at home. Be constantly watching as God is always orchestrating events for us.

2. Realize that it's an emergency.

Matthew 9:36 (The Message Bible): *"When he looked out over the crowds, his heart broke. So confused and aimless they were, like sheep with no shepherd."* Now is the time for action. We notice the event, but often put off action thinking it can wait. Planning is great and a must in life but sometimes we need to prepare for an unseen event before it occurs. An example is keeping money in your wallet at all times assuming God will give you an opportunity to bless someone at any minute.

3. Assume responsibility.

Romans 12:10-13: *"Be devoted to one another in brotherly love. Honor one another above yourselves. Never be lacking in zeal, but keep your spiritual fervor, serving the Lord. Be joyful in hope, patient in affliction, faithful in prayer. Share with God's people who are in need. Practice hospitality."*
Stop assuming someone else has a plan. Take action and get involved. We have all heard stories of people taking action, believing they were going to bless someone, only to hear them tell how God actually blessed them instead.

4. Know what to do.

Job's friends just came and sat with him for seven days. They did not talk or tell him what to do. They simply sat with him. The key is Job had friends who knew him well, they had taken steps to be part of his life. When times were difficult for Job, they knew exactly what to do because they had spent time with him.

Do you have someone in your life who will just show up? Are you spending time with others so you will be ready when their time of need comes?

_____

_____

_____

5. ACT!

Luke 15:3-7 (NIV): *"Then Jesus told them this parable: 'Suppose one of you has a hundred sheep and loses one of them. Does he not leave the ninety-nine in the open country and go after the lost sheep until he finds it? And when he finds it, he joyfully puts it on his shoulders and goes home. Then he calls his friends and neighbors together and says, "Rejoice with me; I have found my lost sheep." I tell you that in the same way there will be more rejoicing in heaven over one sinner who repents than over ninety-nine righteous persons who do not need to repent.'"*

Jump in the water to save those drowning and stop assuming someone else is going to help. Take action when God speaks to you. Be generous, not because you have to, but rather because God has been generous to you. For a sheep to be lost it usually meant it was trapped and in danger. The sheep needed help, not planning or hope. It needed to be rescued. There are sheep all around us who need to be rescued. We have the opportunity to leave those who are safe and step into the trap or danger of those who are lost. Like the Shepherd in the story, we also have the great opportunity to rejoice when a lost or endangered sheep is rescued. We are not meant to be locked away with our sheep in the churches, but rather we are to be out in the fields looking for those who are trapped or in danger.

What lost sheep are you aware of in your life today?

_____

_____

_____

How can you ACT today to make a difference?

_____

_____

_____

Words to live by: *"Do to others as you would have them do to you." (Luke 6:31)*

Day 7   Pray

As fathers, we are to pray for our families. Jesus, our role model, was in constant communication with God the Father. In fact, the Bible tells us that Jesus didn't say ANYTHING he didn't hear his father saying, and he didn't do ANYTHING that He didn't see the Father doing. And he received all of that intel from heaven through prayer. Prayer was such an important part of Jesus' life that everything he said and did was an outflow of his communication with God. Our lives are to be the same. First Thessalonians 5:16-18 tells us, *"Rejoice always, pray without ceasing, give thanks in all circumstances; for this is the will of God in Christ Jesus for you."*

But what if you don't know how? What if no one ever taught you how to pray?

Too often, we overcomplicate spiritual matters like prayer and miss the simplicity of it. Prayer is simply talking to God and telling him what's on our heart. It's taking Bible verses and personalizing them, praying them back to him. Here's a simple example:

God, thank you for today. Thank you for my family. I pray the protection of Psalm 91 over them today. Because of your Word, I believe that you are our refuge and our fortress, our God in whom we trust.

Now, take the time to write out your own prayer.

_____

_____

_____

_____

_____

_____

_____

_____

Words to live by: *"The earnest prayer of a righteous person has great power and produces wonderful results" (James 5:16).*

WEEK FOUR

Becoming a Warrior

"Adversity toughens manhood, and the characteristic of the good or the great man is not that he has been exempt from the evils of life, but that he has surmounted them."
–Patrick Henry

Protecting what is ours requires us to stand up to the enemy of this world—and standing up to the enemy demands we develop the warrior within. It requires that we know who our real enemy is: *"For we do not wrestle against flesh and blood, but against the rulers, against the authorities, against the cosmic powers over this present darkness, against the spiritual forces of evil in the heavenly places" (Ephesians 6:12).*

To fight an enemy who seems invisible, who isn't flesh and blood, requires faith and prayer. It requires we develop the priest within first and then the warrior God has called us to be.

God has given every man a territory to protect—and he has done so since the very first man, Adam: *"The Lord God took the man and put him in the Garden of Eden to work it and take care of it (protect it)" (Genesis 2:15).* As Adam was faithful, he entrusted to him more. He gave him tasks to complete, like naming all the animals. Eventually, he saw it fitting to give him a companion, and he fashioned Eve (Genesis 2:21-25). Adam's world grew from being responsible for just himself to being responsible for tasks, a territory and a wife.

Our greatest challenge is learning that to protect our territory is not something we just do, but it is a lifestyle we must live. Protecting our territory is to be at the core of who we are. Whether we're single or married, young or old, protecting our territory is a lifelong responsibility. It's what men do. It's how men love. It's how increase comes. The key to becoming a fully grown man, to powerful manhood, is fully owning, taking responsibility for, tending, standing guard over, and assuring the healthy condition of the territory assigned to you.

Being a warrior is a fulltime job and a way of life. It's a never-ending road of self-discovery and self-improvement, one in which we are continually trained and tested so we can be ready for the enemy's surprise attacks—physically, mentally and emotionally. So, if you don't mind, stand up with me, and let's talk about the traits you'll need to join the warrior class!

Day 1   Deal With Doubt And Unbelief

So many men whine and complain about their sins. They make excuses for their failures, addictions and shortcomings, but refuse to do anything about them. Don't just bellyache about your sin—kill it!

> *"Be killing sin, or sin will be killing you."*
> *–John Owen*

As warriors, we need to learn to make war. There is something about war that sharpens the senses. You hear a twig snap or a rustling of the leaves, and you're in attack mode. Someone coughs, and you're ready to pull the trigger. Even after days of little or no sleep, war keeps us vigilant.

There is a mean, violent streak to the true warrior man. It's a violence against all lust in our own selves, all enslaving desires for food, alcohol, sex, pornography, money, the praise of man, power, fame, racism, hatred, indifference to justice, indifference to poverty—THOSE things are our enemies!!

Ephesians 6:12: *"For our struggle is not against flesh and blood, but against the rulers, against the authorities, against the powers of this dark world and against the spiritual forces of evil in the heavenly realms."*

We tend to think of spiritual warfare as this thing where you find some way to pray or lay hands on someone against a "Satan thing"—and that's important. But it's not nearly as important as this: The only foothold that Satan has in your life is the foothold **you** give him in your mind.

Nobody goes to hell because of Satan. The only reason a man goes to hell is because of sin. Satan isn't your biggest enemy. He doesn't have that kind of power. Your biggest enemy is your mind. It's time to make war against the things that look to entangle you.

Take a moment to write down areas of your life where the enemy of your mind is winning.

_____

_____

_____

_____

Hebrews 12:1-2: *"Therefore, since we are surrounded by such a great cloud of witnesses, let us throw off everything that hinders and the sin that so easily entangles. And let us run with perseverance the race marked out for us, fixing our eyes on Jesus, the pioneer and perfecter of faith."*

Matthew 11:12: *"From the days of John the Baptist until now the kingdom of heaven suffers violence, and violent men take it by force."*

2 Corinthians 10:3-6: *"For though we walk in the flesh, we are not waging war according to the flesh. For the weapons of our warfare are not of the flesh but have divine power to destroy strongholds. We destroy arguments and every lofty opinion raised against the knowledge of God, and take every thought captive to obey Christ, being ready to punish every disobedience, when your obedience is complete."*

Romans 12:2: *"Do not be conformed to this world, but be transformed by the renewal of your mind, that by testing you may discern what is the will of God, what is good and acceptable and perfect."*

Our experience has shown us that mental toughness can be trained and that mentally tough people achieve extra-ordinary success in every area of life.
The ancient Greeks understood and embraced the concept of using hard training to develop the mind, along with the qualities of good citizenry, such as discipline, honor, integrity, teamwork, fortitude, and compassion.

Alabama Coach Nick Saban talks all the time about mental toughness and how much his team needs it. Exactly what is his definition of mental toughness?

"I think mental toughness is a perseverance that you have when you can make yourself do something that you really don't feel like doing. In other words, you don't really feel like getting up, but you get up. You don't feel like practicing today, but you practice. You don't feel like focusing today, but you focus. And, even in difficult circumstances and difficult surroundings, you can stay focused on what you need to stay focused on. So, it really is a mental discipline to be able to stick with in whatever circumstance you are in, and continue to persevere at a high level, and not let some other circumstance affect how you perform."—Nick Saban

Mental toughness affects everything you do. And the first step to becoming mentally strong is to know the truth. John 8:32: *"Then you will know the truth and the truth will set you free."*

In war, it is REALLY important to know:
- Which side you are on
- Who the enemy is
- The objective of your mission
- What role you play in the success or failure of the mission
- What it will take for the mission to be a success

When you know who you are and whose you are, you will know what to do. Then all that's left to do is develop the discipline required to do it.

The Bible calls Satan the "Father of Lies." His greatest weapon against you is unbelief and doubt. If he can keep you from the truth, then he can stop you from achieving victory in your life.

What areas of your life are being limited by doubt and unbelief?

_____

_____

_____

1 Peter 5:8-9: *"Be alert and of sober mind. Your enemy the devil prowls around like a roaring lion looking for someone to devour. Resist him, standing firm in the faith, because you know that the family of believers throughout the world is undergoing the same kind of sufferings."*

You have to begin the battle against sin with the truth.

The only way to know who you are is to know who God is, because your true identity can only be found in Him. Once you know the truth of who you are, then it's important to call for back-up.

Ecclesiastes 4:9-10: *"Two are better than one, because they have a good return for their labor: If either of them falls down, one can help the other up. But pity anyone who falls and has no one to help them up."*

On a team, we operate in the complex world of "others" rather than the relatively simple world of "me," because that forces us to up our game.

You need to be engaged in more challenging activities to accomplish the task—such as planning, goal setting, coordination, and leveraging the team's assets—while simultaneously covering for weaknesses, being held highly accountable, and risking exposure of your own weaknesses.

There's a big difference between working out and training. Training is about using our bodies in the same manner that we operate. This is why IAM4 is so important. In the IAM4 movement, it isn't just about learning some new concepts and philosophies about manhood, and then going home and doing nothing. It is about applying those principles in "real life" situations. We're going to do work. We're going to practice what we preach. But it all starts with challenging your mind. Know the truth. Be disciplined. Be mentally tough.

Words to live by: *"Do not be conformed to this world, but be transformed by the renewal of your mind…" (Romans 12:2).*

Day 2   Get Mentally Tough

The battlefield against sin really does start in your mind—so the battle must be won in the mind first. But you can't win any battle in your mind until you learn to be mentally tough. Here are some steps to becoming mentally tough:

1.   Stay POSITIVE

Humans have two basic choices in every situation: We can focus on that which is good about the situation or that which is bad. If you want to feel badly about yourself, start focusing on everything that's not going your way: your last performance review at work, the weather, your finances, your aches and pains. If you want to feel good, however, all you have to do is to focus on the excitement of life, the number of people that support you and want you to succeed, or the opportunity that failing presents for you to learn something about yourself. You don't need a reason to feel good about yourself. You don't have to earn it like you do money. You can simply choose to fill your mind with energizing, optimistic thoughts.

List areas in your life where you have been focusing on the negative:

_____

_____

_____

List areas in your life where you have been focusing on the positive:

_____

_____

_____

What do you think makes the difference in the two lists above?

_____

_____

_____

2. Have a short MEMORY

To be mentally tough, you have to learn to let things go. If you allow yourself to become bogged down by past bad performances, you will never be able to move forward toward better current and future performances. It's similar to driving a car: If you drive while only looking in the rearview mirror, you are certain to crash. Where will you crash? Into the future—that which is in front of you. Rearview mirrors are there to use when backing up—temporarily—and to notice what is behind you while driving forward. In life, this means that you acknowledge your past failures or falls, and then learn from them so that you do not repeat them. After all, everybody fails. Toughness means that you know this, but do not allow yourself to dwell on those past failures.

What past failures are you holding on to that you need to release or move on from?

_____

_____

_____

3. Become a RITUAL-AHOLIC

Rituals serve to soothe and calm us. They bring us back to the familiar. Think about how you wake up in the morning: I'm sure you have a ritual that you perform like most mornings, like brushing your teeth, showering, and turning on the TV. That is because human beings are creatures of habit. The better the habits, the better the results.

4. Hang around WINNERS

If you want to get great at basketball, then do you go down to the local playground and go for a pick-up game with some first graders? Or do you go downtown to the courts where the big boys hang out and jump in the game? Do you head to the gym on a Friday afternoon or do you head out to the local bar for Miller Time with Joe and the boys? To get better, you have to work out with—and hang around—those who are at or above a level where you want to be.

To get mentally tough you have to do the same. Get in an environment where only the tough survive, and you will see your mental conditioning rise after the first day. The Bible says in Proverbs 27:17, that iron sharpens iron, so metal sharpens metal. You get tough by getting next to those people who are already at the next level.

What do you need to add "winners" to your life?

_____

_____

_____

5. Visualize the FUTURE

That's right—get a mental picture of how you want to be in your future self. In order to get through this current situation or circumstance, you have to not only survive—but also thrive. Think of your future self and how it will feel to be debt-free. Think about the peace you'll feel when your car breaks down and you'll have the money in savings to pay for it. Use details to create a positively charged emotion that your mind will connect with.

Mental visualization is key. Before the championship game, athletes like Michael Jordan rehearse the winning shot, playing it over and over in their minds as they practice and shoot baskets. Michael Jordan pictures himself cutting down the basket from the winning game. Tiger Woods sees himself putting on the green jacket at Augusta Nationals.

What do you visualize that you will put in your mind to help carry you through the rough and bumpy road?

_____

_____

_____

You have to BEGIN with the END in mind!

Words to live by: *"Now faith is the substance of things hoped for, the evidence of things not seen" (Hebrews 11:1).*

Day 3   Gain Emotional Control

Emotional control is a reflection of depth of character:

2 Peter 1:5-9: *"For this very reason, make every effort to supplement your faith with virtue, and virtue with knowledge, and knowledge with self-control, and self-control with steadfastness, and steadfastness with godliness, and godliness with brotherly affection, and brotherly affection with love. For if these qualities are yours and are increasing, they keep you from being ineffective or unfruitful in the knowledge of our Lord Jesus Christ. For whoever lacks these qualities is so nearsighted that he is blind, having forgotten that he was cleansed from his former sins."*

Our bodies are giant energy producers and storehouses. The energy we store is often emotional "baggage" which ideally should not have been stored to begin with. With stored emotional baggage, the day comes when that energy comes back to haunt us as fear, anger, timidity, jealousy, rage, a scarcity mentality, and other negative beliefs and responses.

Take a moment to write down any emotional baggage you are currently carrying around with you today:

_____

_____

_____

Galatians 5:16-24: *"But I say, walk by the Spirit, and you will not gratify the desires of the flesh. For the desires of the flesh are against the Spirit, and the desires of the Spirit are against the flesh, for these are opposed to each other, to keep you from doing the things you want to do. But if you are led by the Spirit, you are not under the law. Now the works of the flesh are evident: sexual immorality, impurity, sensuality, idolatry, sorcery, enmity, strife, jealousy, fits of anger, rivalries, dissensions, divisions."*

Galatians 5:22-23: *"But the fruit of the Spirit is love, joy, peace, patience, kindness, goodness, faithfulness, gentleness, self-control; against such things there is no law."*

It should be our desire to develop a still of mind. As stillness of mind develops depth of thought and sincerity, so stillness of emotions forges depth of character.

Think of a stream: In the places where it is shallow, the water is choppy and turbulent, much like our "monkey minds." But in places where the water is deep, there is stillness and calm.

Psalm 46:10: *"Be still, and know that I am God; I will be exalted among the nations, I will be exalted in the earth."*

In practical terms, this means we have stilled our minds and emotions; hence, we have cultivated the ability to separate ourselves from both internal and external distractions.

If we are prey to our stored negative emotions, when someone pushes our buttons, then we will fail in our ability to focus clearly on the situation, to listen with our whole being, and to respond powerfully.

How do we work on emotional control?

TRANSPARENCY!

For some that may be therapy, and in the IAM4 movement we have battle buddies!

John 1:5: *"The light shines in the darkness, and the darkness has not overcome it."*

Like the proverbial monster that disappears when the light is turned on, negative stored emotions can be flushed out simply by shining the light of awareness on them. Being real with your battle buddy is paramount if you want to achieve any level of emotional health.

If you're starting to store up negative emotions and you're being open with a group of men or one man who loves you, then the likelihood of you letting those emotions go is so much greater than if you're doing life alone.

Being still doesn't mean you aren't moving. It means you're moving forward in peace. If you can't control your emotions, then you will never know true peace. You'll be driven by doubt and worry, disbelief and fear.

Philippians 4:6-7: *"Do not be anxious about anything, but in every situation, by prayer and petition, with thanksgiving, present your requests to God. And the peace of God, which transcends all understanding, will guard your hearts and your minds in Christ Jesus."*

3 Reasons We Lack Emotional Control

1) We lack SELF-AWARENESS

Developing self-awareness is like learning to read a weather barometer. With practice, you can tell whether the barometric pressure is rising or falling, predicting either smooth sailing or storms ahead. Similarly, with a little effort, you can learn to identify how you are feeling. Once you can accurately understand what you are feeling, you then can learn to take steps to control and even influence how you feel. As you increase your self-awareness, you will better understand how things impact you, and how you can gain increased control over your emotions. Being AWARE of your emotions is the first step to controlling them!

Rate your Self Awareness on a scale from 1-5 (1 being none, 5 being totally aware)

_____

_____

_____

What steps do you need to take to improve your score?

_____

_____

_____

2) **We have a negative SELF-IMAGE**

Self-image is the personal lens through which we view ourselves and the world around us. A self-image that is positive, i.e., we genuinely feel good about and like ourselves, is a key component of emotional strength. Having a negative self-image is like being divided against oneself, where sometimes you are your own friend, and other times you are your worst enemy. As "a house divided against itself cannot stand," a person with a negative self-image will, intentionally or subconsciously, engage in behavior that is self-defeating or harmful. The key to developing a positive self-image is to not only accept yourself, but also to work toward becoming your "better self." As you make changes to improve yourself and your life, your self-image will improve.

You need to know and embrace how God sees you as opposed to how you see yourself. Grab hold of the promises in scripture and know that God says that EACH ONE of them is yours through Jesus. You are the son or daughter of the Most High God. You are an overcomer. NO weapon formed against you can prosper. You are blessed in the city and blessed in the field. The same power that raised Christ from the dead lives within you. When God looks at you, He doesn't see a worthless sinner. He sees His child, the person He died for.

For the most part my self-image is:

_____ Positive
_____ Negative

Why?

_____

_____

_____

3) **We're UNGRATEFUL**

Gratitude is one of the most important factors in controlling your emotions because the opposite of gratitude is entitlement. You feel like you deserve something or that other people should treat you a certain way.

Grateful persons usually have happier relationships as their family, friends, and co-workers feel appreciated and valued. In addition, cultivating gratitude leads to an abundance mindset where one feels that he or she has everything needed for happiness and success.

Grateful persons are less prone to mental distress because thankfulness for the things that we have minimizes the pain we feel when we lack certain things—especially when we want them very badly. Grateful people are less likely to set arbitrary and often subconscious rules that have to be met before they allow themselves to be happy. For example, I'll be happy when I get married, graduate school, or get out of debt. Having requirements before "happiness" can be experienced is problematic because this tendency always pushes our happiness off into the future. It causes us to not live in the present where it can actually be experienced.

How often do you use words like PLEASE and THANK YOU?

_____

_____

_____

How often do you tell those people closest to you how much you appreciate them?

_____

_____

_____

A grateful heart is the key to controlled emotions.

Words to live by: *"A man without self-control is like a city broken into and left without walls" (Proverbs 25:28).*

Day 4   Be Self-Aware

To achieve total victory, awareness, intuition and sensory development are pivotal. This key element can be broken down into 4 steps:

1) Attention Control

You must become aware of your thoughts and determine whether they are positive or negative. Negative thoughts will sap your physical energy and therefore need to be stopped. Positive thoughts, on the other hand, need to be focused!

Philippians 4:4-9: *"Rejoice in the Lord always; again I will say, Rejoice. Let your reasonableness be known to everyone. The Lord is at hand; do not be anxious about anything, but in everything by prayer and supplication with thanksgiving let your requests be made known to God. And the peace of God, which surpasses all understanding, will guard your hearts and your minds in Christ Jesus. Finally, brothers, whatever is true, whatever is honorable, whatever is just, whatever is pure, whatever is lovely, whatever is commendable, if there is any excellence, if there is anything worthy of praise, think about these things."*

Think about an electrical charge. Are you positively charged or negatively charged?

_____

_____

_____

What negative thoughts do you need to move away from in your life?

_____

_____

_____

2) Body Control

You must learn to control your body and not let your body control you.

1 Corinthians 6:19-20: *"Or do you not know that your body is a temple of the Holy Spirit within you, whom you have from God? You are not your own, for you were bought with a price. So glorify God in your body."*

1 Corinthians 9:24-27: *"Do you not know that in a race all the runners run, but only one gets the prize? Run in such a way as to get the prize. Everyone who competes in the games goes into strict training. They do it to get a crown that will not last, but we*

do it to get a crown that will last forever. Therefore, I do not run like someone running aimlessly; I do not fight like a boxer beating the air. No, I strike a blow to my body and make it my slave so that after I have preached to others, I myself will not be disqualified for the prize."

In what areas of your life does your body control your responses rather than your mind?

_____

_____

_____

3) Concentration

Focus on THIS MOMENT RIGHT NOW! If you allow yourself to worry about the future, or what's next, you can easily become overwhelmed.

Matthew 6:25-34: *"Therefore I tell you, do not worry about your life, what you will eat or drink; or about your body, what you will wear. Is not life more than food, and the body more than clothes? Look at the birds of the air; they do not sow or reap or store away in barns, and yet your heavenly Father feeds them. Are you not much more valuable than they? Can any one of you by worrying add a single hour to your life? And why do you worry about clothes? See how the flowers of the field grow. They do not labor or spin. Yet I tell you that not even Solomon in all his splendor was dressed like one of these. If that is how God clothes the grass of the field, which is here today and tomorrow is thrown into the fire, will he not much more clothe you—you of little faith? So, do not worry, saying, 'What shall we eat?' or 'What shall we drink?' or 'What shall we wear?' For the pagans run after all these things, and your heavenly Father knows that you need them. But seek first his kingdom and his righteousness, and all these things will be given to you as well. Therefore, do not worry about tomorrow, for tomorrow will worry about itself. Each day has enough trouble of its own."*

4) Meditation on the Word

Meditation isn't some weird thing where you sit on the floor and chant, "Ohmmmm." Meditation is defined as: The discipline to listen deeply absent of active thought.

Meditation is where you see it before you see it—where you see it before you do it. If you don't see it before you see it, then you will never see it. You and I meditate all the time. The problem is we typically concentrate on negative thoughts, so we reap negativity. Mark Divine puts it best when he said, "What the mind believes the body achieves."

Psalms 19:14: *"Let the words of my mouth and the meditation of my heart be acceptable in your sight, O Lord, my rock and my redeemer."*

It's all about learning to keep our mouths shut, to keep our minds open, and to listen with our whole being.

John 10:27: *"My sheep hear My voice, and I know them, and they follow Me."*

In your own words describe your time meditating on God's word. What does your quiet time consist of?

_____

_____

_____

Words to live by: *"Search me, God, and know my heart; test me and know my anxious thoughts. See if there is any offensive way in me, and lead me in the way everlasting." (Psalm 139:23-24)*

Day 5   Get Physically Fit

Most men are less "manly" than they should be due to the culture we live in. We are being told that we need to get rid of anything that is considered a "gender indicator" under the guise of equality. Boys are told it's OK to play with either Barbie® dolls or trucks. Men and women are able to use the same restrooms at the same time. It is not that difficult to see that culture's entire thought process is out of balance. Maybe at this time you have come to the realization that you are out of balance. Here are just a few things to do to move toward embracing the warrior spirit in you:

1) Get Physically Fit

Being physically fit does not mean that you need to have muscle on top of muscle or be able to run a marathon. But there is a physically fit version of yourself that you should be able to enjoy.

All males who strive to step into manhood should workout. Taking a brisk walk in the mall does not count as a workout. Do something that causes you to breathe heavy and sweat. If the brisk walk in the mall does that for you now, then start there but don't stay there. Don't be afraid to push yourself. If you puke, then that's a good indicator that you're getting closer to being a warrior!

2) Develop Routines

Developing routines is vital for not only warriors but also for mankind as a whole. We are what we repeatedly do. Sadly, most men do not have a routine. Most men are sporadic because their days, weeks and lives are sporadic. The lack of a routine makes you feel like you can't gain any ground in life.

Start establishing routines and habits in everything you do. Get up at a certain time, and go to bed at a certain time, even on vacation. Read and study the Word of God at the same time every day. Eat healthy at the same times every day. Exercise a certain number of days a week at the same time. Warriors know the value of a routine.

Have a consistent routine of:
- Reading
- Writing
- Relationships
- Exercise
- Diet
- Rest

3) Have a Vision

The Bible teaches that people are unrestrained without a vision. People need to know where they're going in life. Otherwise, you will live with no direction and do whatever seems right in the moment without considering the impact and consequences of your decisions in the future.

Males that want to reach manhood understand the importance of having a vision for their personal lives. Consider where you want to be mentally, emotionally, physically, and spiritually, and then develop a plan to get there. Develop a vision for your ideal marriage, family life and career. Consider how you want your relationship with God to grow. Create an attainable vision, but don't sell yourself short. God is able to do more in your life than you can even imagine, but you must start striving for it.

Take some time and write down your goals in each of these areas and review them once a month.

_____

_____

_____

_____

If you don't have a map for your life, how can you expect to get where you want to go?

4) Compete

All males need to embrace competition. Society is afraid of hurting people's feelings so little league gives out trophies for first, second, third and fourth place—and sometimes they don't even keep score! We are losing the art of competition. Competition is where a man finds out what he is made of. In early history, this was a regular practice. The Romans used to battle each other for public entertainment in the Coliseum. There is a reason little boys challenge each other to foot races and wrestling matches. Competition is a part of manhood.

As males moving into manhood, we should still sign up for a race or challenge someone to arm-wrestle. Prove that you're better than someone else at something, or work until you are better than them!

When was the last time you challenged another man to any type of competition? What was it and how did it turn out?

_____

_____

_____

5) Be a Winner

"No one is born a loser or a winner but we are all born choosers."

–Keith Craft.

Many men excuse themselves from being winners because their dad, mom, or other family members were losers. But the opposite is true also. Some men think that because my dad, mom or family were winners, I will be a winner, too. Both of these thought processes are fatal because no one is born a winner or a loser. We are, however, born with the ability to choose.

You must understand this truth. You cannot live differently than you believe. Choose to believe you are a winner, then be a winner. Do the things winners do. Everything in life is either worth doing well or it's not worth doing at all. You are a winner!

6) Get Hit!

Do you remember the first time you ever got hit? Do you remember the shock that took over your body after getting punched? Take a moment to write out the facts you remember from that event:

_____

_____

_____

You knew you should be kicking this person's ass but instead you were frozen. At some point you engaged in the fight, but you hesitated a few seconds before you reacted.

The reason you had a delayed reaction is because you had never been hit before.

Do you remember the first time you had the wind knocked out of you? Do you remember the fear that came over you and the sound you made like a cat dying? You thought you were dying, and your dad or coach or some other male walked over to you, at which point you looked up panicking, trying to ask for help, but nothing came out except the dying cat sound. Then the man you were looking at to save you shoved you down and screamed, "JUST BREATHE!" He grabbed you by the front of your pants and pulled you up and down. A few seconds passed by and you finally caught your breath, realizing that you weren't going to die.

Now, the truth is you did not have the literal wind knocked out of you. In actuality, you suffered a blow that threw your diaphragm into a spasm making it difficult to breathe. When you could not manage to breathe, you panicked. The reason you panicked is because you had never had the wind knocked out of you before and you didn't know what to do. But after it had happened the first time, the next time you remained calm and said to yourself, "I'm not dying. I'll be fine, just breathe. And in a few seconds you were fine.

I'm startled by the increasing number of males who have yet to be punched in the face or have the wind knocked out of them. At the very least go get punched in the face! Start practicing some form of fighting art like MMA, karate, boxing, or jujitsu. Just pick one you like and go get punched in the face a few times, and find out what it means to have the wind knocked out of you.

If you have never been punched in the face, then when your enemy comes around, it startles you to the point that you freeze or flee. Freezing is NEVER okay. You need to know what it is like to make a decision after the first punch has been thrown. A warrior can make right decisions even under pressure. If you've never been hit, then you don't know how to get back up. Just like when the wind has been knocked out of you, once you know how to respond in tough circumstances, you are able to remain calm and get up the next time.

You may think this to be silly, and that's fine. Just know that life will hit you so hard it knocks you down and knocks the wind out of you. As a man, you can't just lay there with a look of terror and shock on your face thinking you're going to die. The people around you need you to lead the way and get back up! As Rocky said, "It's not about how hard you can hit. It's about how hard you can get hit and get up!"

7) Decision Time

Before we go any further, we need to make a decision. Most men know how to make excuses, but in this moment, I want us to make a decision.

Everyone is one decision away from a different life. It is too easy to blame our current situation on people and circumstances, but when we do, we are failing to see the common denominator in all of life's situations—ourselves. If you want to change your life, you must change what you believe. It is decision time. If you want a different life, then you must make the decision to change the way you live. You must believe that the concepts and truth that you are learning are what you must implement to have the life you desire. Don't believe these principles to just be good ideas. Allow them to change you so that you can change your life.

Words to live by: *"May God himself, the God of peace, sanctify you through and through. May your whole spirit, soul and body be kept blameless at the coming of our Lord Jesus Christ" (1 Thessalonians 5:23).*

Day 6   Develop a Never Quit Attitude

The strongest weapon in the war against our flesh is a never give up attitude! A never give up attitude encompasses all aspects of physical, mental, emotional, and spiritual development.

How do you attain an unbeatable spirit?

1) Practice TOTAL PRESENCE. Be 100 percent in the here and now.

Isaiah 43:18-19: *"Remember not the former things, nor consider the things of old. Behold, I am doing a new thing; now it springs forth, do you not perceive it? I will make a way in the wilderness and rivers in the desert."*

The future and the past do not exist in the present. The past is a memory. The future is a notion. By collapsing time to the present we eliminate uncertainty and analysis paralysis.

"Wherever you are, there you are."

We have all heard people complain about being in the wrong place at the wrong time. BUT THAT CAN'T HAPPEN! Wherever you are, there you are. You are either at the right place at the right time—meaning you are present—or you are at the right place at the wrong time—meaning that your head is in the past or future. In either case, the decisions you make at that moment will determine whether you are a loser or a hero. When you practice total presence, you will have the mental toughness and clarity for right thoughts, and right thoughts ALWAYS lead to right decisions.

2) Eliminate FEAR

"Courage is resistance to fear; mastery of fear–not absence of fear."
–Mark Twain

Fear exists in the gap between what we know to be true, and what we don't know to be true. The wider the gap, the larger our fear.

Part of eliminating fear is practicing total presence. But on top of that, you also must seek to "close your openings." That means we must overcome weaknesses that can open us up to critical failure.

We don't need to master everything in life, just the important things.

The ULTIMATE way to eliminate fear is to practice NON-ATTACHMENT. If you're not attached to loss, then you don't fear losing. Paul said to LIVE is Christ, to DIE is gain (Philippians 1:21). The only thing Paul was attached to was God. There was NOTHING in this world that would hold him back. You can't beat someone that doesn't have anything to lose.

What fears do you have today that you have attached yourself to?

_____

_____

_____

3) Practice HYPER-FOCUS.

Hyper focus is focus to the exclusion of everything else. Once focused on an action, or goal, you place ALL your emotional, cognitive, subconscious and action energy toward achieving that goal.

Hebrews 12:1-3 "Therefore, since we are surrounded by such a great cloud of witnesses, let us throw off everything that hinders and the sin that so easily entangles. And let us run with perseverance the race marked out for us, fixing our eyes on Jesus, the pioneer and perfecter of faith. For the joy set before him he endured the cross, scorning its shame, and sat down at the right hand of the throne of God. Consider him who endured such opposition from sinners, so that you will not grow weary and lose heart."

4) Total COMMITMENT.

Worthy pursuits are not taken on lightly with an air of "maybe." There is no room for hesitation, and there is no turning back. You do not have a Plan B! No compromises. No quitting. Pain is temporary; quitting is forever.

Where do you have "Plan B's" in your life today?

_____

_____

_____

What are these Plan B's stealing from the Plan A's?

_____

_____

_____

What we're talking about is LIFE or DEATH. War isn't a game, and the life we're living is most definitely a war that carries eternal significance!

There is a scene in "The Empire Strikes Back" where Luke Skywalker is standing on the edge of a swamp as his X-wing fighter sinks ever deeper into the muck. Yoda encourages Luke to use the Force to lift the ship out of the swamp, but Luke is frustrated. He weakly offers back, "OK, I'll give it a try."

Yoda responds sternly: "NO! Try not! Do, or do not. There is no try!"

Luke fails. Yoda proves him wrong. In the end of the next movie they blow up the unfinished Death Star, which for some reason has a fatal flaw in its design that allows a single shot to generate a chain reaction that destroys it.

There have been moments in all our lives when we, like Luke, were standing on the edge of the swamp offering up a wimpy, "OK, I'll give it a try." In many ways, these moments were more about self-protection than about accomplishment. We wanted to ensure that if we failed, then we had an insurance policy, an escape clause.

"Try" was our escape clause.

If I "try" something and fail, it wasn't really my fault. Maybe the project was too big, maybe it wasn't really "my thing" or maybe there were other factors conspiring against me.

But if I attempt to do something with all I have and I fail, then there is a good chance that I'll have to stare at my own limitations and deal with my mortality. I'll have to face the fact that I'm not as capable as I wish I were or imagine that I am.

In life, we don't want to have to deal with our limitations any more than we want to think about the possibility of death. So, we shrink back, and fly into battle to offer up some halfhearted attempt at victory, but all the while we have our finger on the eject button!

What we're talking about is serious. SIN NEVER SLEEPS! You don't get to walk out on the fight because the fight is on your doorstep.

Grab hold of the words of Master Yoda, "Try not! Do, or do not. There is no try!" It's time we all listen to the CALL OF DUTY! It's time we all MAKE WAR!!

"Adversity toughens manhood, and the characteristic of the good or the great man is not that he has been exempt from the evils of life, but that he has surmounted them."
–Patrick Henry

Perspective changes things. Jesus is a conquering king and warrior. For humanity and the church, Jesus comes mounted on a donkey, a beast of peace. For His enemies, however, He is a divine warrior who comes on a white horse with a sword of judgment, leading the army of heaven behind Him to rescue His people. He is our hero! The Bible confirms Jesus as warrior on multiple occasions:

- Exodus 15:3: *"The Lord is a warrior the Lord is his name."*
- Isaiah. 42:13: *"The Lord goes out like a mighty man, like a warrior he stirs up his zeal; he cries out, he shouts aloud, he shows himself mighty against his foes."*
- Psalm 18:34: *"He trains my hands for war, so that my arms can bend a bow of bronze."*
- Psalm 144:1: *"Blessed be the Lord, my rock, who trains my hands for war, and my fingers for battle."*

As men, we are called to imitate the warrior characteristic as Jesus. As warrior, you are to fight for and protect those things that you hold most dear. Embracing the warrior characteristic is essential to your journey of manhood. If you don't get being a warrior right, then you can't function as prophet, as priest, or as king. As a warrior, you must protect what is yours. This requires you to stand up against the enemy of this world.

- Ephesians 6:12: *"For we do not wrestle against flesh and blood, but against the rulers, against the authorities, against the cosmic powers over this present darkness, against the spiritual forces of evil in the heavenly places."*

You are in a spiritual battle! You must be aware. You must fight the spiritual battle through faith and prayer. You can't teach the Word to people, pray for a family, serve people or even manage something that you have allowed the enemy to come in and destroy.

As a Warrior, what are the things you hold most dear in your life?

_____

_____

_____

Being a warrior is a fulltime job and a way of life. You need to be trained and tested so you can be ready for the enemy's surprise attacks. The way of the warrior is a never-ending road of self-discovery and self-improvement.

Words to live by: *Jesus replied, "No one who puts a hand to the plow and looks back is fit for service in the kingdom of God" (Luke 9:62).*

Day 7 Develop Your Non-Negotiables

All males everywhere need to grow a set of NUTs:

Non-negotiable

Unalterable

Terms

NUTs are values we're not willing to compromise in life. But, I caution you: It is not enough to say we have values. We must actually live by them. The bigger the sack of Nut's we have, the more of a warrior we will become!

The following is a list of **7 Non-negotiable Unalterable Terms** I encourage you to live by. The first word in each one is the value you must possess, and the following two words are the virtues that are displayed when the value is lived out.

1. Freedom = Self-Control & Discipline

A warrior values freedom; therefore, the virtues a warrior must possess to acquire freedom are self-control and discipline.

A warrior of the past, present and future, will always need self-control and discipline. Therein is where greatness lies, growth occurs, and freedom is found. Discipline is not a picture of perfection but a picture of excellence as the warrior strives for perfection. Discipline is defined by my ability to do the things I hate in order to have the things I want.

What disciplines should you incorporate into your life?

_____

_____

_____

When you do incorporate these into your life, what will you gain that you want?

_____

_____

_____

Self-control, discipline and responsibility are the weights of freedom that true men carry—and warriors carry these burdens gladly. God has created you to be a warrior, and a warrior knows God has not called him to a life of ease or mediocrity. He knows that God has called him to a life that goes beyond anything he could dream or imagine, and he knows it is a worthy pursuit (Ephesians 3:20). He knows to let go of the things behind him and lay hold of the prize before him (Philippians 3:14).

2. Relationships = Polite & Right

A warrior knows there's nothing more important in life than quality relationships; therefore, he will cultivate the virtues necessary to produce relationships: being polite and choosing right.

Being polite is the expression of a benevolent regard for the feelings of others. Therefore, a polite man does not walk into a room and attempt to make everyone feel less than. No, he will be courteous and act like a warrior who walks into a room and "owns it" because of his humble confidence in God. As a warrior, he will go out of his way to make people feel comfortable.

A true man also knows the value of *right* relationships. While he will make himself approachable to anyone, he will not hang out with everyone. *"If you want to grow in wisdom, spend time with the wise. Walk with the foolish and you'll eventually become just like them" (Proverbs 13:20).*

A true man values three types of *right* relationships in his life: his mentor, those he mentors and his friends.

His mentor: This is someone who has gone before him and values his beliefs, core values and achievements in life.

Those he mentors: A true man looks forward to passing on his own experiences and wisdom as well the wisdom he is gleaning from his own mentor.

His friends: Proverbs 18:24 says, *"A man of many companions may come to ruin, but there is a friend that sticks closer than a brother."*

A true man knows in order to be friends with someone we must have four things in common:

1) Morals which are standards or beliefs concerning what is right and wrong.
2) Values which are foundational beliefs that are the bedrock of who you are and that are precious to you.
3) A Code of Ethics which is how you operate socially and deal with social issues.
4) The same Stage in Life which is where he is professionally, relationally—married, single, kids or no kids—and in wisdom.

3. Excellence = Consistency & Determination

A warrior has a deep value for excellence, and it is shown in his life through the virtues of consistency and determination. Why these two virtues? Because anyone can do something well one time, but a true man understands the power in a determined and consistent life of excellence.

Doing things with excellence requires an ability to adapt to any given situation. Marines use the phrase, "Adapt and overcome." Life will throw you circumstances that you cannot foresee. Your ability to "adapt and overcome" will determine your success as a warrior and as a leader.

A warrior is sure of himself. He is a winner; therefore, there is little hesitation in his decisions.

A warrior has the gift of assertiveness. He is willing to speak up with his ideas and viewpoints. He fights for what is right. He fights for justice.

4. Servanthood = Humility & Honesty

A warrior has a heart of service, and it is portrayed through the virtues of humility and honesty. Serving others is our greatest opportunity to be an expression of Jesus to people—and when we serve with humility and are completely honest with them, we're giving them our best. When we respond to their questions with truth, when we confront behaviors they need to change, we are living as true servants. But when we lie, or hedge the truth, perhaps because we don't want to hurt them, we rob them of their ability to grow and to make a decision rooted in truth.

5. Honor = Loyalty & Submission

Honor is doing the hard thing when it is the right thing, even when the easy thing is right in front of your face, especially when no one is looking, when no one would know which path you chose.

Honor is knowing what you would die for, and until a man knows what he will die for, he cannot fully live.

So how do you develop honor?
- *Never cheat to get ahead.*
- *Always help someone in need.*
- *Never compromise your values. Ever.*
- *Never be, or see yourself as, a victim.*
- *Never stab a man in the back even if he's done it to you.*
- *Always honor the position/authority over you.*
- *Never gossip or be OK with gossip.*

6. Power = Courage & Strength

If you have the courage to face your demons, your fears and the world, then you are a warrior. When you live a life of power, it will be seen through the virtues of courage and strength. Often people teach that courage is not being afraid, when actually, it's the exact opposite. Courage is being afraid yet doing the task at hand anyway.

While all men have the capacity for courage, the challenge for many men is that courage cannot be accessed until commitment is made. Most men want courage in order to make a commitment, but we must make a commitment to gain the courage.

It is ironic to me that as kids we didn't *practice* courage. And when we got into trouble or did something stupid, we practiced fear and weakness, and most of our parents enabled it. They made excuses for us rather than forcing us to man up and own our mistakes.

When was the last time you had to own up to your mistake?

_____

_____

_____

How did it make you feel?

_____

_____

_____

Did you see value in owning up to your mistake?

_____

_____

_____

7. Generosity = Mercy & Grace

A warrior values generosity, and generosity is shown through the virtues of mercy and grace. Mercy is defined by not getting what you deserve, and grace is defined by giving you more than you deserve. Warriors understand that being generous is also investing their time, talents and money into God's kingdom. They do not shy away from the word tithe nor the understanding that tithing is not being generous, but tithing is only doing what is required.

- A warrior doesn't fight for his own gain, but for his family, church, nation, friends, and fellow warriors.
- A warrior's lifestyle screams mercy and grace.
- A warrior knows the value of life.
- A warrior is unselfish and has compassion for others.

Words to live by: *"All you need to say is simply 'Yes' or 'No'; anything beyond this comes from the evil one" (Matthew 5:37).*

WEEK FIVE

Becoming A Prophet

"A man does what he must—in spite of personal consequences, in spite of obstacles and dangers, and pressures—and that is the basis of all human morality."
– John F. Kennedy

Suggesting you imitate Jesus by being a prophet can sound a little intimidating to say the least. It might just scare the crap out of you. Chances are you have never made a statement including the phrase, "Thus sayeth the Lowerd." If you have, then I am sure there is a book for you, but this is not it. Don't let the idea of being a prophet cause you to pull back. Just take a deep breath. Relax. And trust me that being a prophet is simpler than you think.

As you look into the Scripture and begin studying the role of a prophet, you will see that God, in his wisdom, chose men who would obey him faithfully—so the first step in developing the prophet within is to just be obedient.

Then, God gave those obedient men the authority to speak on his behalf.

Day 1   Be Obedient

Prophets were not chosen or elected by men but by God. Prophets were not permitted to inherit their title or regard it as an official post to be filled by specially trained men. There were no strenuous prerequisites to be a prophet, because it didn't really require any special knowledge or skill. God just told them what to do and what to say—and that's what he'll do for you.

With no real special knowledge or skill required, I bet you're feeling qualified already. If all you have to do is what God tells you, being a prophet gets a lot less stressful. The Bible references the work of a prophet in numerous places, but to give you an idea of what they were supposed to do, let's take a look at three:

1) God speaks through the voice of the prophets. Deuteronomy 18:18-19 says, *"I will raise up for them a Prophet like you from among their brethren, and will put My words in His mouth, and He shall speak to them all that I command Him."*

2) God reveals His plans to the prophets. Amos 3:7 says, *"Surely the Lord GOD does nothing, unless He reveals His secret to His servants the prophets."*

3) God uses prophets to lead and protect his people. Hosea 12:13 says, *"By a prophet the LORD brought Israel out of Egypt, and by a prophet he was preserved."*

In order to teach the things of God and to lead as God is directing you, then you must be a serious student of the Word so you will know God's voice when he speaks—and God has made that easy as well.

What is the last thing God told you to do?

_____

_____

_____

Were you obedient? Did you do it?

_____

_____

_____

Day 2   Examine Your Heart

Though found in early Sanskrit texts, I am not sure who actually wrote the following quote, but I like it:

"Watch your thoughts, they become words. Watch your words, they become actions. Watch your actions, they become habits. Watch your habits, they become character. Watch your character for it becomes your destiny."

Thoughts ⇉ Words ⇉ Actions ⇉ Habits ⇉ Character ⇉ Destiny

This is good news and bad news at the same time. You are where you are in life at this moment because of decisions that you have made. Your decisions were determined by your thoughts. The Bible really is true. Proverbs 23:7 says, *"For as a man thinks in his heart so he is."*

Most of us spend our lives focusing on the mere symptoms of a heart issue. What is sad is we have failed to understand that the thing that shapes our hearts is not something out of our control. Our heart is the one thing you can control. The things you think on most often shape your heart.

This put in one word is meditation. Ask yourself these questions:

What do I read?

_____

_____

_____

What do I spend time watching on TV?

_____

_____

_____

What am I listening to?

_____

_____

_____

What kinds of people do I hang around?

_____

_____

_____

Who have I given permission to speak into my life?

_____

_____

_____

Once you have answered these questions you will be able to determine what is shaping your thoughts, and you will know exactly why you are where you are. God wants you to experience abundant life! Two Questions:

Is your life producing what you want?

_____

_____

_____

Is your life producing what God wants?

_____

_____

_____

One of the greatest things you can do for yourself, your family, your church, and your community is to learn how to study God's Word.

Words to live by: *"Keep this Book of the Law always on your lips; meditate on it day and night, so that you may be careful to do everything written in it. Then you will be prosperous and successful" (Joshua 1:8).*

Day 3   Begin to Study the Bible

We hear a lot about the fact we need to study the Bible, but it's as if no one wants to take the time to teach us how to study the Bible.

If the Bible is—and it is—the most important book ever written, and if it is—and it is—the book that contains the Words of God, then it would just make sense, common sense even, that we would be taught how to study it.

I am going to give a three-step process to help you study God's Word so you can be confident when you teach, speak and live out His Word as a Prophet.

Step 1: Observation

Observation is the first and most important step in the process. As you read the Bible, you need to look carefully at what is said and how it is said. Look for:

• **Terms, not words** - Words can have many meanings, but terms are words used in a specific way in a specific context. (For instance, the word trunk could apply to a tree, a car, or a storage box. However, when you read, "That tree has a very large trunk," you know exactly what the word means, which makes it a term.) The same is true in the Bible. In biblical times, they used words to mean different things depending on how they used them in a sentence. For us to grasp an understanding of what is being communicated, we have to see terms not just words.

• **Structure** - If you look at your Bible, you will see that the text has paragraphs. A paragraph is a complete unit of thought. You can discover the content of the author's message by noting and understanding each paragraph. It has been said that we should read one line above and one line below to gain full understanding.
That is a great start, but even in doing that you can pull something out of context, which will cause you to misunderstand what God is saying.

• **Emphasis** - The amount of space or the number of chapters or verses devoted to a specific topic will reveal the importance of that topic.

• **Repetition** - This is another way an author demonstrates that something is important. One reading of 1 Corinthians 13, where the author uses the word "love" nine times in only 13 verses, communicates to us that love is the focal point of these 13 verses.

Read Psalm 23, applying these 4 observation techniques. Write your findings:

Terms, not words:

_____

_____

_____

Structure:

Emphasis:

Repetition:

Words to live by: *"But whose delight is in the law of the LORD, and who meditates on his law day and night" (Psalm 1:2).*

Day 4   **Observe the Relationship Between Ideas**

Pay close attention, for example, to certain relationships that appear in the text:

1. **Cause-and-effect:** *"Well done, good and faithful servant; you were faithful over a few things, I will make you ruler over many things" (Matthew 25:21).* This action will cause this action. Because you did this, this is going to happen in effect.
2. **Ifs and thens:** *"If My people who are called by My name will humble themselves, and pray and seek My face, and turn from their wicked ways, then I will hear from heaven and forgive their sin and heal their land" (2 Chronicles 7:14).* If you do this, you need to know this will happen.
3. **Questions and answers:** *"Who is the King of glory? The Lord strong and mighty" (Psalms 24:8).* What I find exciting about the Bible is often God will ask a question and answer His own question to keep us from guessing.

• **Notice Comparisons and Contrasts.** For example, *"You have heard that it was said…but I say to you…" (Matthew 5:21).* The Bible will often contrast assumptions or cultural norms with truth.

• **Pay Attention to the Literary form.** The Bible is literature made up of:
  1. Law (Torah)
  2. History
  3. Poetry/Songs
  4. Wisdom Sayings (Proverbs)
  5. Gospels
  6. Letters (Epistles)

Considering the type of literature makes a great deal of difference when you read and interpret the Scriptures. Take Song of Solomon 7:3 for example where it says; *"Your breasts are like two fawns, like twin fawns of a gazelle."* Now I believe the Bible is absolutely true without error. But I in no way think or even believe that the writer's wife had a set of twin gazelles sitting on her chest. We know that Song of Solomon is a book of poetry, and poetry uses strong imagery to communicate a point.

• **Think About the Atmosphere.** The author had a particular reason or burden for writing each passage, chapter and book. Be sure you notice the mood or tone or urgency of the writing.

After you have considered these things, then you are ready to ask: Who? What? Why? When? Where?

- Who is writing this passage?
- Whom is it written to?
- What is happening in this passage?
- Where is this story taking place? In a town, city or countryside? And in which geographical location?
- When in time is it? Time of the day, of the year, in history? This gives you cultural significance.

Asking those additional questions for understanding will help to build a bridge between observation—the first step—and interpretation—the second step—of the Bible study process.

Begin to capture the answers to the questions above in your personal journal.

Using Psalm 23 again, examine it in light of these additional study techniques.

Words to live by: *"Study to shew thyself approved unto God, a workman that needeth not to be ashamed, rightly dividing the word of truth" (2 Timothy 2:15).*

Day 5   Learn How to Interpret Passages

Interpretation is discovering the author's main thought or idea in a passage which reveals the meaning. Answering the questions that arise during observation will help you in the process of interpretation. Use the Five C's to help you determine the author's main point(s):

- **Context.** By considering context, you can answer 75 percent of your questions about a passage when you read the text. Reading the text involves looking at the near context—the verse immediately before and after—as well as the far context—the paragraph or the chapter that precedes and/or follows the passage you're studying.

- **Cross-references.** Let Scripture interpret Scripture. That is, let other passages in the Bible shed light on the passage we are looking at. At the same time, let's be careful not to assume that the same word or phrase in two different passages means the same thing.

- **Culture.** The Bible was written long ago, so when we interpret it, we need to understand it from the writers' cultural context.

- **Conclusion.** Having answered our questions for understanding by means of context, cross-reference and culture, now we can make a preliminary statement of the passage's meaning. Remember that if our passage consists of more than one paragraph, the author may be presenting more than one thought or idea.

- **Consultation.** Reading books known as commentaries, which are written by Bible scholars, can help us interpret Scripture.

Always remember that you cannot appreciate the content without understanding the context. Look at a couple of your favorite scriptures, maybe ones you have memorized, and look at them through the 5 C's of Interpretation. Or, you can review Psalm 23 once more. Journal any thoughts or new understanding God gives you on these verses.

Words to live by: *"The person without the Spirit does not accept the things that come from the Spirit of God but considers them foolishness, and cannot understand them because they are discerned only through the Spirit" (1 Corinthians 2:14).*

Day 6   Apply the Word to Your Life

Application is why we study the Bible. We want our lives to change, and we want to be obedient to God and grow more like Jesus Christ. After we have observed a passage and interpreted or understood it to the best of our ability, we must then apply its truth to our own life.

You'll want to ask the following question of every passage of Scripture you study:

- *What is/are the timeless principle/principles in this Scripture?*

In light of that answer, ask these questions:

- *How does that affect my relationship with God?*
- *How does that affect my relationship with others?*
- *How does that affect me?*
- *How does that affect my response to the enemy, Satan?*

The application step is not complete by simply answering these questions. The key is putting into practice what God has taught you in your study.

Putting into practice what God has taught you is done by meditating on what you have just studied and giving it time to change you. We have already stated that you cannot live differently than you believe. Meditation is the way you allow God's Word to be hidden in your heart so that you may not sin against God (Psalm 119:11). Allow what you study to infiltrate your mind throughout the day. Recite what you have learned when you are facing a tough situation. Memorize scripture so that you can always be on guard. But, I caution you, once you read it, you are accountable for it. James 1:22 reminds us of this: *"Do not merely listen to the word, and so deceive yourselves. Do what it says."*

Of the Scripture God has lead you to this week, what has changed in your life by adding the step of "Application" to your Bible study?

_____

_____

_____

Words to live by: *"But be doers of the word, and not hearers only, deceiving yourselves" (James 1:22).*

Day 7   Become a Teacher

The best teachers are the ones who lead by example and create a culture that is contagious. As we develop the prophet within, we need to understand that part of a prophet's role is to teach.

We're to teach our families first—to be their primary teacher of the things of God. We can't push off that responsibility to the church and then get mad when things don't work out like we wanted them. That's never OK. As the prophet of our lives and homes, it is our sole responsibility as a man to teach our families, to speak of the things of God and to lead as we believe God is directing our families. In order to discern God's voice and direction, we must be serious students of the Word. When we hear God's voice and read his instructions, we must live them out. We can speak to our wife and children about the importance of church, prayer, Bible study, loving God, and loving others, but we must also bear the fruit of these actions.

Second, we're to teach other men. It is both the spoken and the unspoken words to men from other men that shape a culture of manhood. How many times have you heard these statements:

- If "so and so" was any kind of man he would do "such and such"…
- Seems to me a man needs to talk with that ol' boy…(and we all know what "talk" means)…
- A man would know what to do…
- You're better than that…

I know some of you are thinking, *Well, I didn't have a man in my life. My dad left when I was little.* I don't mean to be to forward, but that's nothing more than an excuse. It is time for some un-fathered men to stop waiting around for someone to father them. I understand that sounds harsh, but those of us who didn't have a male figure in our lives cannot be tempted to sit around hoping one day an older wiser man will swoop down and impart to us the secret of life. It's not likely to happen.

While we wait, we'll miss the opportunities in front of us. We will miss out on the role we can play in the world. God has placed us on this earth for a purpose. There's only one thing to do—man up. Rise up and be a victor instead of a victim. Learn quickly. Time is slipping, and a new generation of boys is waiting for our example. Let's be the men we wished we would have had to look up to when we were growing up. Let's read God's Word. Then study it and teach it. Let's be the prophet God has called us to be and show ourselves a man.

How can you incorporate teaching into your family time?

_____

_____

_____

How can you incorporate teaching into reaching out to other men?

_____

_____

_____

Words to live by: *"And the things you have heard me say in the presence of many witnesses entrust to reliable people who will also be qualified to teach others" (2 Timothy 2:2).*

WEEK SIX

Becoming A King

"There are two questions a man must ask himself: The first is 'Where am I going?' and the second is 'Who will go with me?' If you ever get these questions in the wrong order you are in trouble."
–Sam Keen

When it comes to our calling as king, we are called to imitate the true servant nature of King Jesus, the one and only King of Kings. King Jesus never ruled with his own power or strength, but he always submitted to THE King (God the Father). King Jesus represented the rule of God, the justice of God, the compassion of God, and the righteousness of God. He gave his life for his people—and when a king dies for his subjects, it doesn't say much about the subjects, but it does say a lot about the king.

We're to imitate Jesus if we want to be a good king. He had absolute power, but he equally had the presence of humility. He had no room for selfishness or greed because a king must always–ALWAYS—love and nourish his kingdom (his home). Like Jesus, a good king must put his people first, be loyal to them and not be afraid of battle. He willingly leads his people on—and commands respect. He knows what is best for his people.

In essence, he rules well. In the New Testament, men are charged with being the head: *"For the husband is the head of the wife even as Christ is the head of the church, his body, and is himself its Savior" (Ephesians 5:23)*. The implication of being the head in the original Greek text literally means "to stand out on front" or "to stand at the head of." Essentially, this means that the father, the man, is the head of his home. He is out on front, he sets the example and he stands in between his family and all the dangers and pressures of life. It means he is the king—and he has what it takes to fulfill his role: great courage. It means he fulfills his responsibilities to have a vision for his family, he knows and communicates the rules of his household, and he makes wise judgments.

Day 1   Communicate Your Vision

One of the main roles of a king is communicating the vision of your kingdom. As a man, your kingdom is your home, so it's your responsibility to lead the way in communicating the vision of your home to everyone in your household. Having a vision is essential to knowing where you want to lead your family: *"Where there is no vision, the people are unrestrained," (Proverbs 29:18).*

Your vision is simply the answers to questions like:

Why does your kingdom exist?

_____

_____

_____

What does your kingdom value?

_____

_____

_____

What will your kingdom stand for?

_____

_____

_____

What will your kingdom NOT stand for?

_____

_____

_____

What does your kingdom hope to accomplish as it moves forward?

_____

_____

_____

Words to live by: *Then the LORD replied: "Write down the revelation and make it plain on tablets so that a herald may run with it" (Habbukuk 2:2).*

Day 2   Determine the Laws

Kings were instructed to "study God's Law and make it their rule." As a king, we are to lead our homes according to what is written in Scripture. We are not to lead based on what is popular or socially acceptable, because that will lead to lawlessness—a condition that grows from a lack of direction and clarity. To have the clarity we need, we will have to create rules, and then live by them.

Here are some questions and thoughts to help us create rules for our homes:

What words will be allowed in our kingdom?

_____

_____

_____

What entertainment (movies and activities) will be enjoyed?

_____

_____

_____

What type of dress will be acceptable in our kingdom?

_____

_____

_____

How will people treat each other in our kingdom?

_____

_____

_____

How will the finances of our kingdom be utilized?

_____

_____

_____

What are the consequences for not adhering to the guidelines/rules in our kingdom?

_____

_____

_____

Remember that imitating Jesus as King means living in love. We are not creating rules for the sake of power and pride. We are creating rules out of love. God gave us guidelines in life so that we can live healthy lives. Like we mentioned earlier, this is not about religion—a list of do's and don'ts—but relationship. As a king, it is our responsibility to provide healthy boundaries for our family because we love them and want what is best for them. Jesus was humble and powerful, but never prideful. He relied on God's wisdom instead of His own. As a king, we must do the same.

Words to live by: *"I know him, that he will command his children and his household after him, and they shall keep the way of the Lord, to do justice and judgement; that the Lord may bring on Abraham that which was spoken to him" (Genesis 18:17-19).*

Day 3   Judge Wisely

As we communicate vision, rules, and guidelines for our kingdoms, we will inevitably have someone test us to see what kind of king we are. They will want to see if we are a tyrant or a slug. They will stir up disagreements and conflicts, and we will have to judge wisely what is the truth and what will stand. We are the sole judge in our kingdom; we have to judge these kinds of matters.

If you are single, then this is somewhat easy. But when you get married and have children, your responsibility as a king will increase. Sometimes men run away from this responsibility in tough situations. They instruct their children to ask their mother about a situation instead.

Now if you choose to exercise your ability to push responsibility onto your wife then there are some things you need to know. A divided kingdom cannot stand. Children are very intelligent and when you, the king, refuse to step into your role, then your beautiful gifts from God will start a very methodical revolution. Your children will start manipulating both parents in order to get what they want.

How do you determine right from wrong?

_____

_____

_____

How will you determine the judgment calls you will need to make regarding your wife and children?

_____

_____

_____

How can you ensure your children will not manipulate you and your wife to get what they want?

_____

_____

_____

Words to live by: *"A kingdom is divided against itself, that kingdom cannot stand"* (Mark 3:24).

Day 4   Manage Your Money Well

If it smells bad, don't eat it. When something smells bad we instinctively know it's not good. I have been a Christ follower for 18 years. Prior to that many people would attempt to "witness" to me, but my thought process was so far from God that religious words and phrases had little to no impact on me.

Twenty years ago, I worked in an environment where my job was to serve and protect the people of a city. During my time there, I interacted with people on a level most people never get to. Often I would find myself trying to help people who were in very difficult circumstances. They were great people trying to care for their families, make ends meet and live life, but it seemed the world was stacked against them. Some may look at them and label them as "poor."

Many of these people were religious and could quote more Bible verses than I knew existed at that time. They would even "witness" to me, inviting me to know God and embrace Jesus as my savior.

This was difficult for me because what they were saying they believed appeared to have zero effect on the life they were living. On one hand, they would quote the scriptures about how God loved them, was providing for them, how they were victorious. How He was their strength and joy, but they had no joy. They constantly were the victim in their situation, and they were usually completely distraught over something.

Then it happened. I met a family that lived in what is known as government housing, and they were altogether different. I arrived because some money of theirs had been taken—money they were needing to pay rent—and without this money they stood the chance of losing their home. Both parents worked, and they had two kids who were in elementary school.

The conversation was the same as with most of these calls. You get the facts first to do your report and almost always the conversation turned religious. Now, I was expecting the same attitude as most. Lots of Scripture quoting with lots of contradictory phrases after.

This was different. They did quote Scripture, but I had already noticed a difference when I pulled up. The yard was clean and well kept. I walked in the house, and it was spotless, and it smelled really good! They had this "air" about them. They seemed happy and confident. All the Scripture they were quoting seemed to make a practical difference. There was no complaining about the loss of money. There was more of an attitude of joy to be able to see what God was going to do.

That family did not lose their house. As a matter of fact, that family moved out of government housing and moved into a very nice rental.

After that encounter, I began to notice something I had never noticed before: SMELLS!

The people I interacted with who had a victim mentality and had no joy—even though they quoted scriptures—I began to notice that there was a distinct smell on them and in their homes.

Shortly after I met the "different" family, I embraced Jesus as my forgiver and leader. It was not until later that I became convinced the scent that was so prevalent in some of those homes was and is related to the spirit of poverty.

Demons are referred to in the Bible as foul and unclean spirits. The definition of *foul* is "to be putrid, offensive and impure." Today, I can detect the same odor that was in those homes in many other homes and on people. My wife and I share the belief that there is a distinct odor that accompanies a spirit of poverty.

Which of these two families do you relate to best?

_____

_____

_____

Are you like family 1? The family who quotes scripture while pointing fingers, finding fault, blaming others or making excuses?

_____

_____

_____

Or are you like family 2? The family who trusts in and believes the scriptures in their lives? The family who walks by faith in life as the scriptures tell us?

_____

_____

_____

What did God reveal to you about yourself as you read about these two families?

_____

_____

_____

Words to live by: *"Suppose one of you wants to build a tower. Won't you first sit down and estimate the cost to see if you have enough money to complete it?" (Luke 14:28)*

Day 5   Eliminate a Poverty Mindset

A person does not need a spiritual gift to detect the traits of the spirit of poverty. For example, in some places, it is common to live in clutter and filth. Christians do not have to call down fire or speak in tongues to get their yard or their house clean. They just clean!

Some will be offended when I talk about this. However, I know from experience that the devil will trick a person's mind to make him or her think living in a cluttered, messy house is normal. I talk often on spiritually and physically cleaning house, and over the years, a few people have felt as if I were picking on them about something they could not help. I understand where they were coming from, but I want to let them know they do not have to stay where they are.

Many people who have lived in impoverished environments and survived on welfare were never taught there is more to life. The spirit of poverty will make you settle for less. I know the signs, and they all add up to what I call "poverty complacency".

Staying on top of everyday issues, such as cleaning house, personal grooming, being on time, maintaining a good driving record, having auto insurance and changing the oil in their cars is not common in the lives of some people. No one has ever taken the time to teach them that these are priorities in life.

They are used to hustling. And when people conform to the environment they have always been exposed to and no one shares or shows them a new way to live, their potential for transformation is destroyed. Without transformation of the mind, there is no transition to the next level.

Numbers 14:24 says that Caleb and Joshua had "another spirit", one that was different from that of the others who were wandering in the wilderness. The word *spirit* in this passage is *ruwach*. One of the meanings of this Hebrew word is "mind".

Joshua and Caleb did not focus on what they were up against in life. They said, "Not only are we able, but we are well able!" (Numbers 13:30). As a result, they went forward to possess what God had promised them.

The other people in the wilderness, even though they had been physically delivered by the same God, had no hope of transition because of their "mindset". After God saves us, we must get a new attitude in order to enter into the fullness of salvation.

Joshua and Caleb saw OPPORTUNITY while the others only saw OPPOSITION.

I understand that people will have challenges in life, but we must consider the vicious cycle of the spirit of poverty and what it robs from us every day.

What opportunities have you abandoned because of a poverty mindset?

_____

_____

_____

What mindset limits you most today?

_____

_____

_____

Words to live by: *"Charge them that are rich in this world, that they be not highminded, nor trust in uncertain riches, but in the living God, who giveth us richly all things to enjoy." (1 Timothy 6:17, KJV)*

Day 6   Break Financial Curses

A sure sign of the poverty spirit is a lot of bills with no provision to pay them. God promises that when He calls you to do something He will provide for it! The problem is people with a poverty mindset will often try to manufacture their own miracle and accumulate things God never said that He would pay for. These financial curses must be recognized and then done away with.

The curse of Cain. Because of Cain's actions—withholding his best offering from God and killing his brother in a jealous rage—he was banished from the presence of the Lord and cursed in his ability to produce a harvest.

Cain was also subject to wander in the land of Nod, east of the Garden of Eden. When we try to hold back on God, we end up with nothing. But Proverbs 3:9 says that if we honor the Lord with all our substance and the first fruits of all our increase, God will fill our barns with plenty.

The curse of Malachi. Malachi 3:10-11 tells us to bring all the tithes into the storehouse. When we obey this principle, God promises to open the windows of heaven over our heads and rebuke the hand of the devourer on our behalf.

Many are plagued with curses because they do not honor God in their tithes and offerings, nor do they obey His teachings about life. These are all holy to God.

Some make the mistake of not obeying God out of love. They only do what God says out of obligation.

Oftentimes, because of this, people do not release their tithes in their minds. Mentally, they follow the money to the offering room, the bank and even the board meeting, worrying about how it is spent.

The word *holy* means "separated to God." Our tithe is not pleasing to God until we have the right attitude about it. The Scripture says to give with joy and the only way to please God is by faith. Faith and joy cannot co-exist with the spirits of fear and poverty.

How do you truly feel about the tithe?

_____

_____

_____

The generational curse of poverty. Exodus 20:5 explains that the iniquities of the fathers can affect as many as four generations.

If the fathers do not listen to the voice of the Lord to do His commandments, poverty is one of the curses that shall be a sign upon their children.

Deuteronomy 28:46 says, *"And they shall be upon you for a sign and for a wonder, and upon your seed forever."*

It is of vital importance that we as parents stop the cycle of poverty. Let me be clear, poverty is not a checking account number; it is a mindset.

Given the book of Exodus tells us that the sins of a father are passed down to as many as four generations, what mindsets were passed to you by your grandparents and parents that do not need to be passed down to your children and grandchildren?

_____

_____

_____

You are the key to breaking the generational mindsets. You must make the decision to move away from tradition and move to the truth.

Freedom from poverty is available to every one of us who is willing to do what God tells us in His Word. If you will start being faithful in your tithes and offerings, if you will honor God's instructions concerning life, honor His house, and seek to pass on a Godly inheritance to the next generation, then you can begin to reverse the curses mentioned, and with God's help, break their power over your life.

As a leader, I feel that my mandate is helping people live life to the fullest. I believe it is a sin to live below the standard that God has given us.

Jesus died so that we would not have to suffer from poverty. When He came to set the captives free, He took the chains off our minds so we would never be slaves to a poverty mindset again.

Words to live by: *"Bring the whole tithe into the storehouse, that there may be food in my house. Test me in this," says the LORD Almighty, "and see if I will not throw open the floodgates of heaven and pour out so much blessing that there will not be room enough to store it" (Malachi 3:10).*

Day 7   You Choose: Poverty or Prosperity

The Prosperity Gospel is a religious belief among some Christians, teaching that financial blessing and physical well-being are always the will of God for them—that faith, positive speech, and giving to religious causes will increase their material wealth. Prosperity teaching views the Bible as a contract between God and humans; that if humans have faith in God, he will deliver security and prosperity. This teaching emphasizes the importance of personal empowerment proposing that it is God's will for his people to be happy.

Poverty Gospel is a religious belief held by some Christians, teaching that God's blessing is found when you are sick and poor. They believe that if you are healthy or wealthy, it is because you do not have enough faith to be used by God, and/or you are in disobedience to God. These Christians teach that only through sickness do you learn to obey God, and only through the refusal of material things can you stay pure in your pursuit of God. To them, true holiness is found in those who constantly struggle.

Let me be clear, in no way do I believe that the prosperity or poverty gospels as presented above are biblical.

Entire false belief systems have been built on single verses of Scripture taken out of context for hundreds of years.

Does God sometimes use sickness and/or poverty to teach us?

_____

_____

_____

Are there Scriptures that state the importance of suffering and being in need?

_____

_____

_____

Is it sometimes God's will for us to go through difficult life circumstances so we can learn from Him?

_____

_____

_____

Does God get pleasure out of blessing His children and seeing them prosper?

_____

_____

_____

Are there Scriptures that promise blessing if we obey God?

_____

_____

_____

Does He use blessing to teach us His faithfulness and goodness?

_____

_____

_____

But, is it always God's desire that we be sick and poor?

_____

_____

_____

Will we never encounter sickness and lack?

_____

_____

_____

It is, however, God's desire that we trust Him, obey Him, and rely on Him no matter the circumstances in our lives.

So, what does IAM4 teach concerning these two viewpoints?

3 John 1:2 says, *"Beloved, I pray that you may prosper in all things and be in health just as your soul prospers."*

Prosper - **2137** *euodóō* - properly, to go on a prosperous journey; to be *on the right (profitable) path*, leading to real success (good fortune) to do well in all areas of life

We strive to teach the whole Gospel!

Does the Bible teach "prosperity"? YES! But it does not teach "poverty".

Before you cut me off, let me clarify. The Bible is concerned with your soul and your spirit. Your soul is your mind, will and emotions. Third John 1:2 says God's desire is that you prosper as your soul prospers. That every area of your life would do well as your mind, will and emotions do well.

John 10:10 says, *"I have come that you may have life and live it to the fullest."*

Perverted poverty and perverted prosperity are both prevalent in the church, and both are spirits that want to destroy your faith and ultimately your soul—your mind, will and emotions.

If the enemy can get you to believe that God only finds favor with those who are sick and without an ability to financially take care of themselves, their families, and His house, then eventually you will be an ineffective Christ follower. That is NOT biblically true.

Likewise, if the enemy can get you to believe that a sign of His favor is only those who are never sick and those who have an abundance of finances, then eventually you will believe God has forsaken you because life is often difficult. That is NOT biblically true.

What is true is the prosperity of your soul—that no matter what circumstances you find yourself in, you are content (Philippians 4:11). That you have joy in hardships (James 1:2). That if you obey God, He will bless you (Deuteronomy 5:33).

You can actually prosper in suffering and lack just as you can prosper in abundance and health. The key is to know that no matter what, God is working all these things for your good (Romans 8:28), and God is blessing you and those around you.

Prosperity is an attitude that comes from a mindset, but, so is poverty. Prosperity has nothing to do with a bank account, just as poverty has nothing to do with a bank account. I know several monetarily rich people who have a poverty mentality. Likewise, I know several people who do not have an abundance of financial resources, but have a prosperity mindset.

People who struggle with a prosperity view of the Bible do so because of three underlying spirits. Yes, these spirits are under everything you do lying to you.

The spirit of fear keeps you from taking risks and causes you to play it safe. It is impossible to experience all that God has for you if you are afraid.

The spirit of guilt causes you to become sinfully self-deprecating. This comes off as extreme humility, but produces ineffectiveness in God's Kingdom, and you will apologize for God's blessing in your life.

The spirit of poverty blinds you from seeing opportunities and causes you to play a victim in your circumstances, leaving you in a personal prison.

Jesus came to set the captives free! I encourage you to examine your faith and see where you land. If you believe a "perverted" Gospel, whether it's one of poverty or one of prosperity, you are not free. The prison you are in is only found in your mind. My prayer is that this study causes you to prosper in your soul. If your soul prospers, so will every other part of your life.

Words to live by: *"The thief comes only to steal and kill and destroy. I came that they may have life and have it abundantly" (John 10:10, ESV).*

IAM4

I lead a men's ministry called IAM4. Since its beginnings, it has grown into a movement seeking to reverse the current trend in our culture by taking men on a journey of self-discovery and self-mastery. IAM4 is a journey that takes a man his entire life to travel. It's not designed so that we arrive, because a true man is always learning and growing. I believe in our day, God has placed a powerful calling on his sons, and within the IAM4 movement we believe it's time for his sons answer the call.

I want to encourage you to surround yourself with men who are striving to restore manhood to its rightful place. Proverbs 13:20 says, *"Walk with the wise and become wise; associate with fools and get in trouble."* As you do this, invite other men to embark on the journey with you.

True manhood has been ostracized by society. Both manhood and society have suffered due to the loss of true men in the world. Men have lost their way and become something they were never intended to become. But together, we can embrace true manhood.

If you would like more information about IAM4, contact me at one of the following:

Email: info@iam4.tv
p. 256-584-7080
Facebook: facebook.com/ivmarsh
Instagram: @iam4.tv

Made in the USA
Middletown, DE
05 September 2020